Nomadic Living

Relocatable Residences

Nomadic Living

Relocatable Residences

Sibylle Kramer

BRAUN

Contents

Preface

Nomadic Living presents a selection of very special homes. Not only in terms of their esthetic qualities and unique appearance, but also because their owners can take them along when moving.

The reasons to opt for a relocatable residence are as diverse as the concepts, construction styles, and designs of these homes. Owners who are in a rush rely on the extremely short construction time made possible by prefabrication and easy transport of the home as a whole or in parts. If they value individuality, they choose a modular design or a one-of-a-kind model. People who are conscious of price stability appreciate that unforeseen cost drivers are nearly non-existent. Finally, those who are still not sure whether they have found the dream location for their small property are glad to know that they can move it at any time.

The 42 relocatable residences shown here are little luxurious gems, which is also in part due to their surroundings as they are usually found in locations with very special views – in the middle of an expansive beautiful landscape, on top of a moutain, on the shore of a lake, in the heart of a forest, or even floating on water. Often designed as artistic structures, they are used as peaceful retreats, as guest or bathing houses, as vacation homes, shelters, or as residences with an individual touch.

Even though the buildings are usually rather small, they offer substantial challenges. Their dimensions are based on the maximum loading width of trucks or the maximum size of the tools with which they are manufactured. The materials are often recyclable with excellent ecological properties. The design of the houses shown here has nothing to do with the image that is provoked by the concept of prefabricated homes.

Designed by skilled architects and designers, these relocatable residences are surprisingly individualistic and uniquely beautiful. The consistent implementation of powerful designs for relocatable homes constitutes an independent field within the residential construction sector. The façades interact with their locations through large glazed surfaces that open up to the surrounding nature or reflect it. They enclose introverted rooms, play with the lightness of filigree structures, or brave the harsh elements with a rugged skin. Due to the construction properties and lightness of wood, this warm material is particularly frequently used.

At the same time, architects and designers are constantly

developing new methods and technologies to meet the owners' demands for fixed prices, short construction times, and the highest quality design. Allow these fascinating pictures and intelligent concepts to inspire and surprise you.

Winter Cabin on Mount Kanin, Slovenia

Architect: OFIS architects
Other creatives involved: CBD structural engineers
Project address: Mount Kanin, Slovenia
Gross floor area: 9.7 sqm
Completion: 2016
Photographer: Janez Martincic

Winter Cabin on Mount Kanin

The challenge of this project was to install real objects, shelters with a scale of 1:1 on remote sites and study their response to extreme weather, radical temperature shifts, snow, and rugged terrain. The harsh conditions of wind, snow, landslides, terrain, and weather require specific architectural forms, structures, and concepts. The site is accessible only by climbing or helicopter – therefore all modules and loads were prepared according to the maximum weight and equilibrium limits.

Its position within the wilderness requires respect of natural resources while ensuring the stability of the shelter with minimal impact on the ground.

Kanin is a mountain above a small town, Bovec, with beautiful resorts around the valley. The area is also the site of World War I battles when soldiers were fighting along the Isonzo front and many remains of the battle can still be found in the area. In collaboration with the Slovenian mountaineer association and PD

Bovec, this particular site was chosen because of its 360-degree views over Slovenia and Italy, and spectacular views of Triglav, Soca Valley and the Adriatic Sea. It will become a destination for hikers, climbers, cavers, mountaineers, nature lovers and romantics.

Kanin Winter Cabin is a compact wooden volume with three floor-resting platforms. These platforms hang towards the valley and a large glazed panoramic window offers astonishing views. A cantilevered overhang, supporting part of the cabin, reaches the smallest footprint on the rock. The interior design is modest, subordinate to the function, and provides accommodation for up to nine mountaineers.

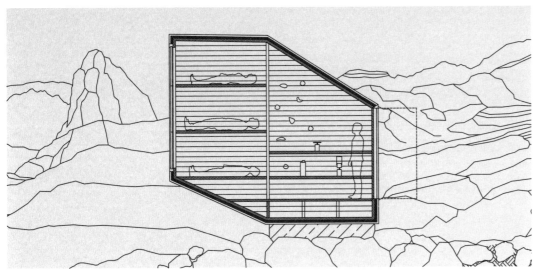

Longitudinal section

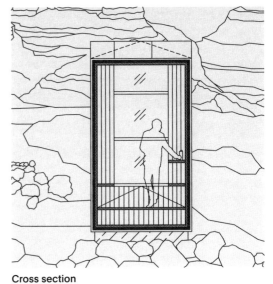

Cross section

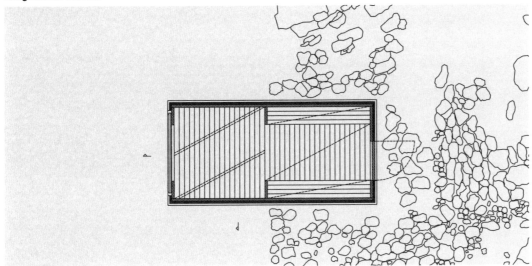

Ground floor plan

Rooms: 1 room with
9 sleeping places
Main materials: timber (CLT),
glass, stone wool, alu panels
Country of manufacture:
Slovenia

Lake Cabin Doksy, Czech Republic

Architect: FAM ARCHITEKTI
Project address: Doksy, Czech Republic
Gross floor area: 42.9 sqm
Completion: 2014
Photographer: Tomas Balej

Lake Cabin

The replacement of an old cabin on a lakeshore in Northern Bohemia respects the unique natural character of the site and follows the cabin's original footprint. The brief of the project was to provide a year-round retreat for the clients' sailing passion, with minimum typology and maximum visual connections to the lake and the surrounding pine forest. The cabin single pitch is a result of internal planning as well as representing the relationship to the lake in which the mooring pier is a principal point of access by boat.

The interior of the cabin is accessed by a large sliding window and designed as a continuous space open to the roof. The tall end includes a sleeping gallery over a compact black box containing the kitchen, toilet, and shower. The principal interior wall forms a deep full-length cupboard for storage with a built-in fireplace. The continuity of the interior is enhanced by the

unifying jangled timber cladding sealed in white oil finish, which gives it a feeling of a cave-like retreat. The floor is sand-colored cement screed reflecting the sandy beach outside.

The focus of the space is on the vast views of the lake and on the relationship of the cabin with its natural surroundings.

The exterior larch cladding reflects the verticality of the surrounding pine trees. One of the practical issues of the project was the safety of the building when not in use. Fixed and folding shutters with identical larch cladding protect the openings and when closed result in a continuous elevation effect.

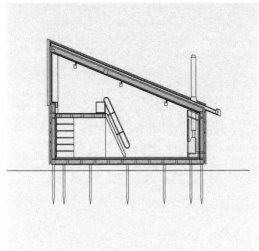

Longitudinal section

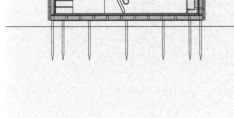

Cross section

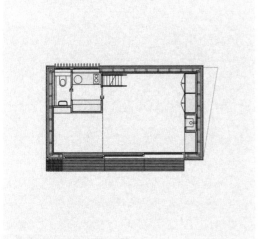

Ground floor plan

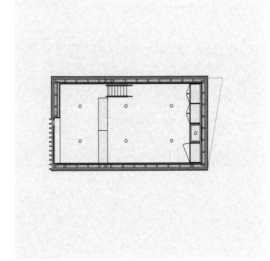

Gallery plan

Rooms: kitchen/living area,
2 bedrooms and 1 bathroom
Main materials: wood
Country of manufacture:
Czech Republic
Building price: 80,000 €

High House
Québec, Canada

Architect: DELORDINAIRE
Project address: Québec, Canada
Completion: 2017
Photographer: Olivier Blouin

For the High House, DELORDI-NAIRE plays with the limit between interior and exterior, inviting people to gather in spaces immersed in nature. Elevated stilt constructions are typically used in warm climates and flood zones. This energy efficient winter chalet uses stilt typology to create a protected ground floor area with an outdoor stove. This provides an unusual space where residents can be amongst nature and the snowy exterior, while still enjoying some protection from the elements.

The stilt typology raises the house above the surrounding tree line, giving it an uninterrupted view of Mont Saint Anne from the lounge, as well as a striking overall esthetic. It also allows sunshine to directly enter the house at all hours of the day. The clean, sharp lines and volumes are achieved using white concrete panel cladding and corrugated steel roof panels. On a cloudy, snowy day, the house blends into the white landscape almost disappearing, and in summer, the minimal white structure cuts a clear form against the surrounding green hills.

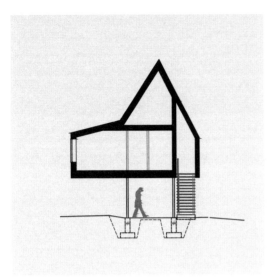

Longitudinal section

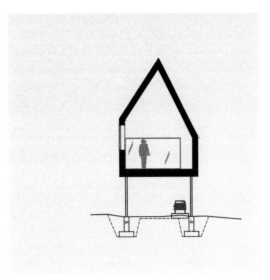

Cross section

Ground floor plan

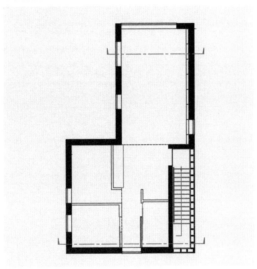

First floor plan

Rooms: kitchen/living area,
2 bedrooms and 1 bathroom
Main materials: white concrete
panel cladding and corrugated
steel roof panels
Country of manufacture: Canada

MIMA Light Viana do Castelo, Portugal

Architect: MIMA Architects
Project address: Viana do Castelo, Portugal
Gross floor area: 21.60 – 32.40 sqm
Completion: 2015
Photographer: Jose Campos

MIMA Light is an iconic object, pure and sophisticated like a minimal art sculpture. The base of the scheme is lined with mirrors, an architectural gesture influenced by the minimalist sculptures of artists such as Donald Judd, John McCracken, and Robert Morris. The rational external design is complemented with comfortable interiors – clad in pinewood and featuring chrome details.

Each unit contains cooking and living spaces, sleeping accommodation, and bathroom facilities. Glass façades provide better ventilation and air circulation, while electricity is located in a centrally positioned core wall, and distributed laterally. An electric boiler connected to solar panels can be installed for heating water. For extremely warm

locations, MIMA recommends using thicker glazing with high UV values.

The entire home is manufactured in a factory before being transported to site. Intended to be simpler to assemble than any previous MIMA product, the house is available in four sizes, ranging from 7.2 meters to 13.2 meters in length. Designed for market sectors that cover tourism, temporary homes, and vacation homes, the dwelling can be distributed to all countries located in the European Union.

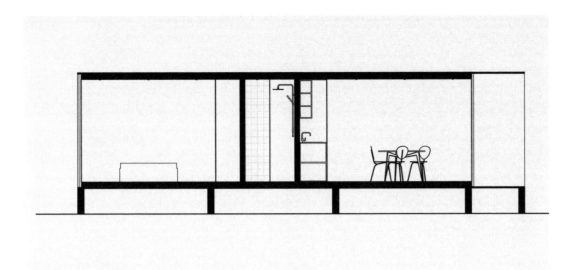

Longitudinal section

Ground floor plan

Rooms: kitchen/living area,
1 bedroom and 1 bathroom
Main materials: aluminum
composite panel, 3-layer pine
panel, mirror glass
Country of manufacture:
Portugal
Building price: 18,875−36,500 €

ÁPH80
Madrid,
Spain

Architect: ÁBATON
Interior design: BATAVIA
Project address: Madrid, Spain
Gross floor area: 27 sqm
Completion: 2013
Photographer: Juan Baraja

ÁPH80

ÁBATON has developed the ÁPH80 series as an ideal dwelling for two people, easily transported by road, and ready to be placed almost anywhere. The proportions are the result of a thorough study by the architects' team, resulting in recognizable various spaces and a feeling of completeness indoors. It is a simple yet sturdy construction made of materials chosen to provide both comfort and balance. ÁPH80 embodies the principles and objectives of ÁBATON: well-being, environmentally sustainability, balance, and simplicity.

ÁPH80 has three different spaces measuring 27 sqm (9×3):

a living room/kitchen, a full bathroom and double bedroom. Its gabled roof is 3.5-meters-high indoors.

Most of the materials can be recycled and meet the sustainable criteria that ÁBATON applies to all its projects. It blends in with the environment thanks to its large openings that bring the outdoors inside.

The use of wood throughout the building not only adds a sense of calm and balance, but is also hypoallergenic. The sourced wood comes from regulated forests that will grow back to provide a wide range of other benefits such as future carbon storage, oxygen generation, and a forest habitat.

Elevations

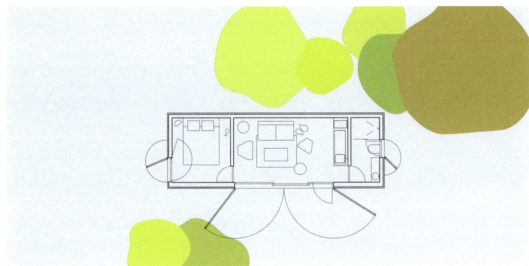

Ground floor plan

Rooms: kitchen/living area,
1 bedroom and 1 bathroom
Main materials: solid timber
structure, outside covered with
gray cement wood board
Country of manufacture: Spain
Building price: from 25,900 €
(Model ÁPH40)

Sol Duc Cabin Washington, USA

Architect: Olson Kundig
Project address: Olympic Peninsula, Washington, USA
Gross floor area: 32.5 sqm
Completion: 2011
Photographer: Benjamin Benschneider

This 32.5 square meter cabin constitutes a small perch for its occupant. When you are inside or on the deck, you are raised up above the landscape with an excellent view out onto the Sol Duc River, while the interior is like a warm dry nest. It is located in one of the few temperate rain forests in the world, and "rain forest" here means wet and rather cold, as opposed to wet and hot. Putting the cabin on stilts protects it from the area's clammy dampness and occasional flooding.

The owner is an avid steelhead fisherman, and the Sol Duc has some of the best steelhead fishing in Washington State. The design allows him and his wife to arrive at this remote location, open the place up, and get to fishing as quickly as possible. The shutters are operated manually via custom steel rods. The large panels slide on hardware that was originally designed for sliding barn doors, attached to the steel roof beam structure.

That it seals up entirely when not in use is important, partly because the location is so remote – with some potential for vandalism – and because the elements can be punishing. Nevertheless, the building is virtually indestructible: it is made of unfinished, mild steel and structural insulated panels. The insides consist mostly of wood, for a sense of warmth.

The materials are a direct response to the surrounding wilderness. Most of the cabin was prefabricated off-site, which minimized construction wastage and site disruption. The loft floor is made from leftover two-by-fours belonging to the owner. The pieces were stacked and glued together, and then bolts were threaded through the stack to secure it.

Sol Duc Cabin

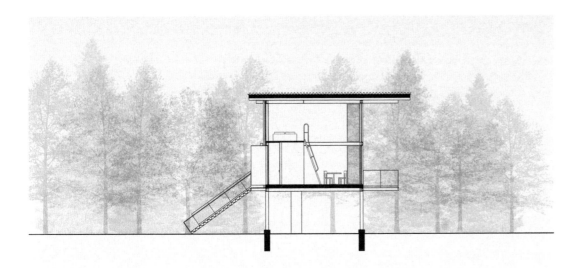

Section

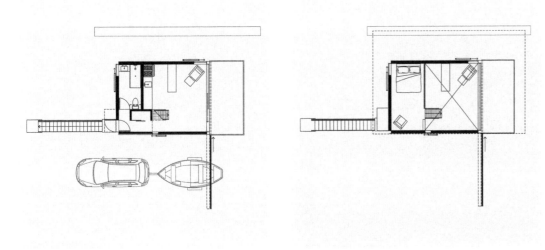

Main level floor plan

Upper level floor plan

**Rooms: kitchen/living area,
1 bedroom and 1 bathroom
Main materials: steel and wood
Country of manufacture: USA**

Blob vB3 Kemzeke, Belgium

Architect: dmvA
Project address: Verbeke Foundation, Westakker, 9190 Kemzeke, Belgium
Gross floor area: 22 sqm
Completion: 2009
Photographer: Frederik Vercruysse

Blob vB3

The design dmvA developed for an extension of the office building of XfactorAgencies was relentlessly rejected by local building regulations.

Used to working with limitations and blurring these boundaries at the same time, dmvA responded by designing a mobile unit, a blob.

As a mobile construction and with a high artistic content, it skirted around the strict building codes.

Blob vB3

The smooth-looking egg consists of a timber frame, which was covered in an elastic material and plastered with polyester. It features various niches and LED lighting. The space between the outer and inner shell was filled with PUR insulation. This space egg houses all necessities of daily life – bathroom, kitchen, lighting, a bed, plus several niches for storage. The nose can be opened automatically and functions as a kind of porch.

The mobile unit is equally suited as an office, a guestroom, a reception, a garden-house, or any other use.

Made of polyester, its size is that of a big caravan and can be moved anywhere. The well-insulated walls, the light-reflecting color white, and the unfolding

segments (cupola and nose), which allow light to enter without direct sunlight reaching the glazed parts behind, contribute to its sophisticated energy concept.

As Flanders is one of the most densely built regions in the world, sustainability is indissolubly linked to the intelligent utilization of land. Small mobile house entities like this project may respond to the lack of open space and green in the form of movable dwelling objects, which can be grouped on the outskirts of towns and villages.

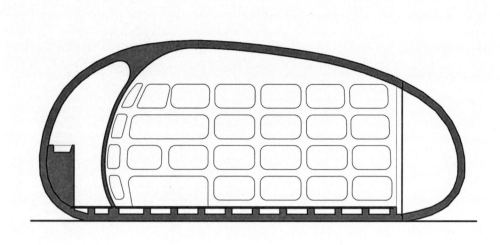

Longitudinal section

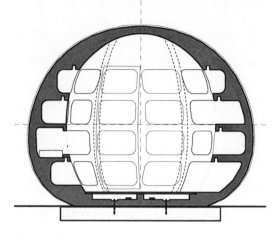

Cross section

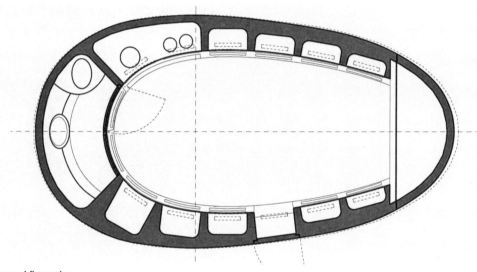

Ground floor plan

Rooms: 1 bedroom and
1 bathroom
Main materials: polyester
Country of manufacture:
Belgium
Building price: 67,000 €

Micro Cluster Cabins Vestfold, Norway

Architect: Reiulf Ramstad Arkitekter
Project address: Herfell, Vestfold, Norway
Gross floor area: 70 sqm
Completion: 2014
Photographer: Reiulf Ramstad Arkitekter

The Micro Cluster Cabins are located at the mouth of the Oslo fjord in the region of Vestfold in Norway. A cluster of pitched-roof volumes sits at the edge of an idyllic meadow in a large clearing. The surrounding woods and a characteristic hill of naked rocks define the site, just a short walk from the sea.

This project was designed for a client who wanted a holiday home for the whole family that could also be somehow divided. This allows them to spend time together but also enjoy the intimacy provided by each part. The solution was a cluster of three structures that can be used individually.

Each building is defined as a clarified geometric volume, organized around the outdoor area that binds them together. All face southwest and the gable end of middle unit is fully glazed, opening it to its surroundings. In the other direction, the buildings are more closed, for privacy from the neighbors and access roads.

The cluster of structures is backed up against a rocky hill creating an exciting spatial interaction between the landscape and the three cabins. The rock mass also creates a beneficial microclimate in the outdoor area: during the day, the sun hits the dark rocks and this heat is gradually released to the environment.

Wood provides a homogeneous cladding for the three structures. The pre-weathered pine heartwood provides a natural look and contrasts with the glazed opening, emphasizing the difference between closing walls. At the same time, the cladding blends in with the environment, keeping the essence and authenticity of the site.

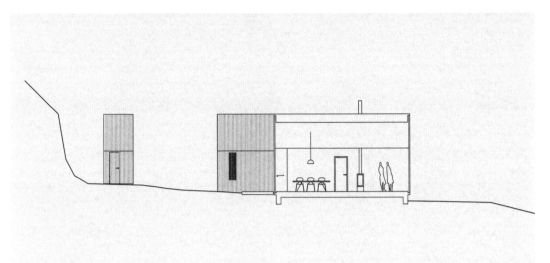

Longitudinal section

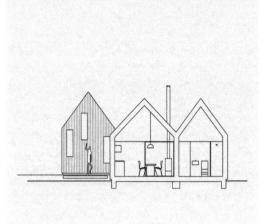

Cross section

Longitudinal section

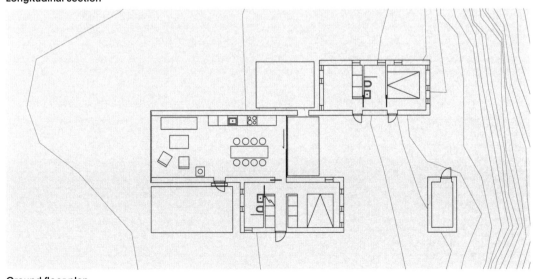

Ground floor plan

**Rooms: kitchen/living area,
2 bedrooms and 2 bathrooms
Main materials: pine heartwood
Country of manufacture: Norway**

DD 16 Moscow, Russia

Architect: Ivan Ovchinnikov, DublDom
Project address: Moscow, Russia
Gross floor area: 16 sqm
Completion: 2015
Photographer: Vlad Mitrichev and
Ivan Ovchinnikov

DD 16

DD 16 is a prototype of modular compact house that was conceived for installation in remote places and extreme conditions. The house consists of two pre-fabricated modules. The prototype was designed and built as tourist equipment with the weight of every detail taken into account so it can be used in very harsh conditions. All the constructive elements and the interior finishing differ from regular houses. The frame is made of laminated wood with milled ports. The ports helped to decrease the weight and prevent cold bridges and gaps. Polyurethane foam is used as an insulation, the rigidity of which helped

to decrease the weight of inner finishing materials. The exterior finishing is made of composite aluminum sheets that form a seamless surface from top to bottom. The internal space features all the potential of compact buildings while offering all conveniences. The large glazing and the great amount of light makes the inside space appear larger.

The same principles are applied to the furnishing – rigidity, weight reduction, and maximum use of space.

The house now is being tested in a rent out format under the DublDomClub aegis. This provides feedback from different people and tests the house as it is intensely used by a great number of customers. An uncommon experience of swimming on a boat and spending a day in a compact floating house is offered to the visitors.

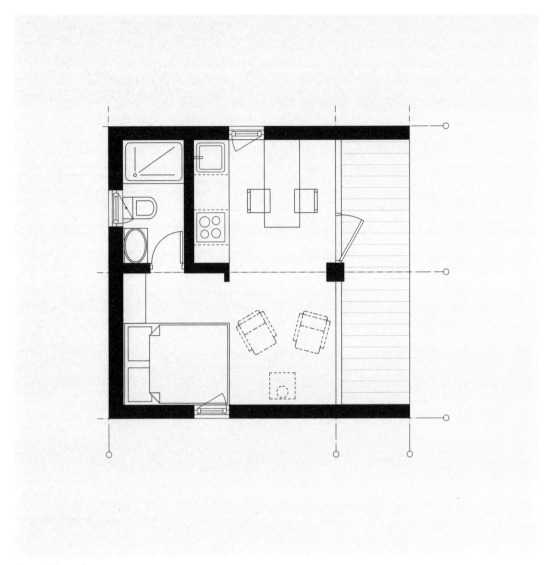

Ground floor plan

Rooms: kitchen/living area
and 1 bathroom
Main materials: wood
Country of manufacture: Russia
Building price: 25,000 €
Modular extensibility: serial
production (www.dubldom.com)

Kokoon Modular Living System Helsinki, Finland

Architect: Aalto University Wood Program
Project address: Helsinki, Finland
Gross floor area: 33 sqm (11 sqm per unit)
Completion: 2016
Photographer: Tuomas Uusheimo,
Juho Haavisto and Anne Kinnunen

Kokoon Modular Living System

Kokoon is a modular living unit built to address the acute shortage of temporary accommodations for asylum seekers, students, and residents displaced by building renovations. The pre-fabricated modules are designed for short term living and can be easily transported and stacked into various configurations to fit different sites in urban and sub-urban contexts. Three prototype units were finished in Helsinki in June 2016 then transported and assembled in various sites around Helsinki. The units can be taken apart, moved by truck, and re-assembled on a new site in one day. The project was designed and constructed by students of the Wood Program at Aalto University's School of Arts Design and Architecture. Design work started in January 2016 and the units were completed in June of the same year.

Rooms: 2 kitchens, 2 bedrooms and 2 bathrooms
Main materials: kerto (spruce LVL) structural frame, sawn spruce cladding, cellulose fiber insulation, solid pine flooring, rhino lining bathroom surfaces, heat-treated aspen bathroom floors
Country of manufacture: Finland

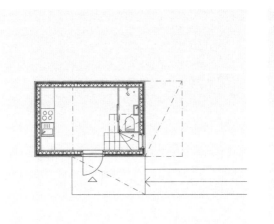

Ground floor plan

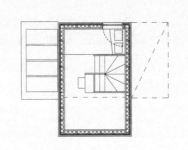

First floor plan

Second floor plan

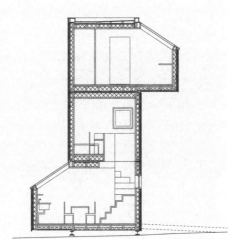

Section

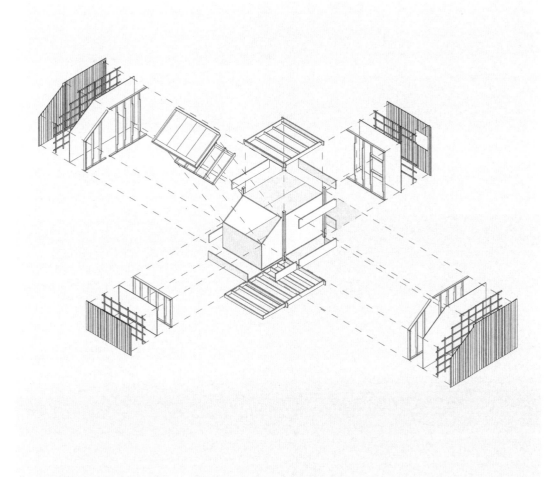

Exploded view

Tarifa House Tarifa, Spain

Architect: James & Mau
Project address: Tarifa, Andalusia, Spain
Gross floor area: 300 sqm
Completion: 2013
Photographer: Erika Mayer

The terrain is located on a slope overlooking the valley that dominates the Strait of Gibraltar. The climate is Mediterranean with hot summers and soft winters, always humid, and very much influenced by the strong winds of Tarifa. The vernacular architecture of Andalusian "pueblos blancos" with their patios and narrow streets reflects how the local building style adapts to the climate. In addition, the client requested not just a mere residential house but a complex that would permit the development of several indoor and outdoor activities.

As a result, the proposal was to condensate a "pueblo" of 300 square meters and turn it into a contemporary "cortijo".

The first characteristic element of a "cortijo" or "pueblo" is the wall that delimitates it. Instead, an open and contemplative enclosure was proposed for this house, created by a huge horizontal plan composed of a permeable, expanded steel mesh pergola.

In the next step, the plan program was exploded, resulting in a series of volumes, just like the buildings or pavilions with different functions that form a pueblo or "cortijo".

The pergola is perforated with as many holes as there are volumes as these are inserted in it. The patios are not fully utilized, leaving the possibility of future additions; after all, a pueblo is not built in a day. The same mesh used for the pergola covers the volumes, creating continuity between them and the fake enclosure. Furthermore, a variety of deliberately empty spaces both inside and outside permits residents to walk in the house on infinite paths, just like in a pueblo.

Tarifa House

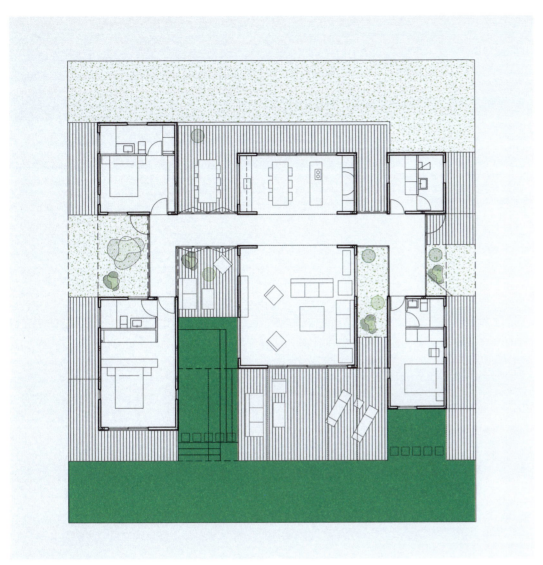

Ground floor plan

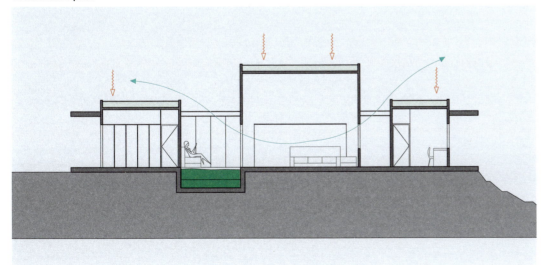

Section

Rooms: kitchen/dining area, living room, 3 bedrooms and 4 bathrooms
Country of manufacture: Spain
Main materials: steel

Houseboat No.1 Belfast, Northern Ireland

Architect: Bluefield Houseboats
Project address: Belfast, Northern Ireland
Gross floor area: 48 sqm
Completion: 2016
Photographer: Bluefield Houseboats

Houseboat No.1

There is something uniquely restful and soothing about being around water. With constantly changing sounds, sights and colors, an environment is both relaxing and invigorating.

It comes as no surprise then that the market for waterfront property is highly competitive and inevitably commands a premium price for those fortunate enough to find a site.

Bluefield Houseboats wants to create innovative, useable space on the water that allows everyone to enjoy this environment. Its mission is to create high-quality, useable space on the water, which is accessible to all and maximizes the use of modern technology to explore sites that have previously been inaccessible.

The featured project was the company's first houseboat, delivered to a private residence in greater Belfast, Northern Ireland, in July 2016. It is a typical 48 sqm / 500 sqft module with two bedrooms, ensuite shower room, and open plan kitchen/living/ dining area. The design also incorporates a perimeter balcony, with glass guarding and external access to a generous roof terrace. Generally, the company's designs do not have a motor and are therefore permanent moorings. However, even though this design weighs in excess of 50 tons, once assembled on the water, it can be easily maneuvered into position where it is ultimately anchored to the bank or a jetty.

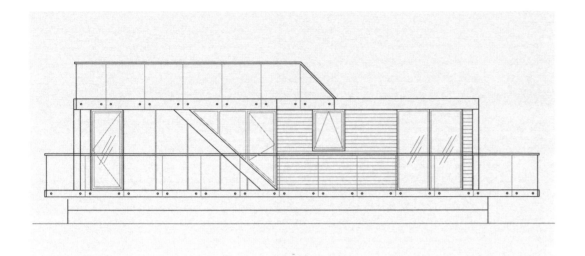

Waterside elevation

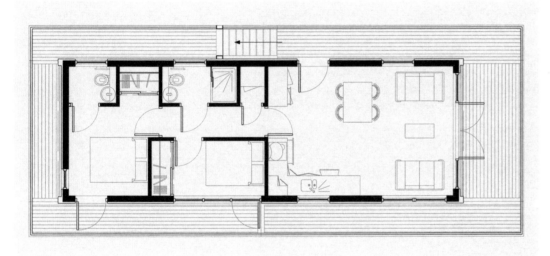

Ground floor plan

Rooms: kitchen/living area,
2 bedrooms and 2 bathrooms
Main materials: timber, steel,
aluminium and glass
Country of manufacture:
Northern Ireland
Building price: 200,000 £
Modular extensibility: design 1
of 4 , ranging from 48–170 sqm
across one or two storeys

minihuset ONE+ Tyresö, Sweden

Architect: Add a Room
Project address: Tyresö, Sweden
Gross floor area: 10, 15, 20 and 25 sqm
Completion: 2011
Photographer: Add a Room, Johan Robach
and Matti Marttinen
Sketches: Lars Frank Nielsen, Architect

minihuset ONE+

Add a Room is a modular mini house concept from Scandinavia, a cooperation between Denmark and Sweden – choosing the best from both countries. The house ONE+ is based on units of 10, 15, 20, and 25 sqm that can be put together in various ways and according to different needs.

The small houses grow by merging the indoors and outdoors. Spacious decks, pergolas, outdoor kitchens, windows with very thin frames, and the same floor lines outside and inside are all carefully chosen to enhance the feeling of outside and inside melting together.

ONE+ house is built with sustainable Scandinavian materials that require minimal maintenance. The thin, outer panel is made of "Superwood" – fully impregnated spruce planks free of heavy metals. The Danish invention offers durability whilst also being sustainable and environmentally friendly.

The house is fully insulated, with energy efficient windows and sliding doors from Velfac. ONE+ is made of Scandinavian wood by skilled carpenters at an indoor production site in Scandinavia and delivered complete in one piece.

All modules are built indoors and transported by truck directly to the plot where they are placed into position by crane. In this way, there is no messy building work on location and the work can take place in all weather conditions.

A small house demands smart solutions, outside as well as inside. Add a Room also offers numerous solutions inside the house, such as wardrobes, beds, and outdoor kitchens.

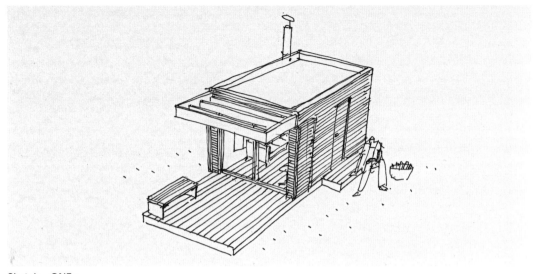

Sketch – ONE +

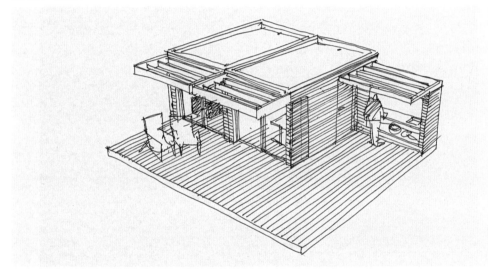

Sketch – 2 X ONE +

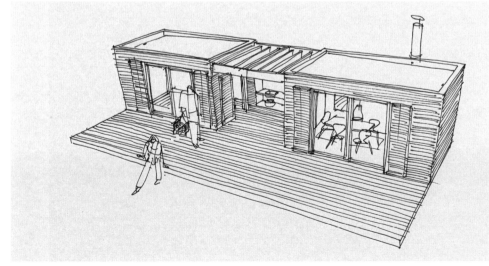

Sketch – 2 X ONE +

Rooms: kitchen/living area,
2 bedrooms and 2 bathrooms
Main materials: Scandinavian
wood
Country of manufacture:
Denmark
Building price: ONE+ modules
starts from 35,000 $
Modular extensibility:
possibility of combining
modules of 10–25 sqm
Special design features:
sustainability in high quality,
minimal maintenance and
constructed in only 12 weeks

Sonoma weeHouse® Santa Rosa, USA

Architect: Geoffrey C. Warner, AIA, Alchemy
Project address: Santa Rosa, California, USA
Gross floor area: 90.12 sqm
Completion: 2016
Photographer: Geoffrey C. Warner, Alchemy

Sonoma weeHouse®

Alchemy's Sonoma weeHouse was designed in Minnesota for a client in San Francisco, built in Oregon, and shipped to its Santa Rosa, California site 90 percent complete.

The client, an architect himself and Apple's Director of Store Design, was the project's co-pilot with weeHouse founder Geoffrey Warner, Alchemy's principal architect. This small, ultra-minimal, high-end home is based on Alchemy's weeHouse but customized to meet the high-end finishing requirements the client requested.

The prefabricated house is composed of two minimalist open-sided boxes set on a concrete plinth nestled on the edge of gnarled oaks and an expansive view. Both structures feature steel frames, 9-feet-tall sliding glass walls set into custom corrugated weathering steel boxes, and ipe wood interiors with oiled oak cabinetry. The boxes are offset on board-formed concrete plinths connected by a set of Alchemy-designed steel stairs and railings fabricated in Minnesota.

The 16 ft. x 40 ft., 640 SF primary box, featuring a whitewashed oak bed box in the middle, creates a kitchen/dining/living room space on one side, and a bath space on the other side. For shipping logistics, the primary box was composed of two modules, with the 10 ft. x 40 ft. porch arriving 90 percent complete, bolted onto the main module on-site, and cantilevered into the site's dramatic landscape. The accompanying 330 SF guesthouse is an abridged version of the larger module with a large whitewashed oak wardrobe forming the bathroom wall.

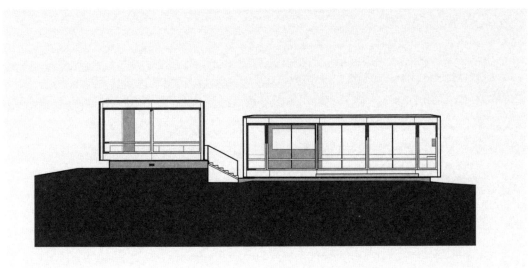

Elevation

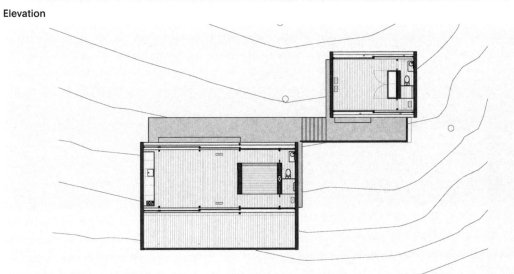

Ground floor plan

Rooms: kitchen/living area,
2 bedrooms and 2 bathrooms
Main materials: wood and steel
Country of manufacture: USA

Colorado Micro-Cabins Leadville, USA

Architect: University of Colorado Denver,
ColoradoBuildingWorkshop
Project address: Leadville, Colorado, USA
Gross floor area: 18.5 sqm per cabin
Completion: 2016
Photographer: Jesse Kuroiwa

Colorado Micro-Cabins

Located on a steep hillside in a pine forest, the Micro-Cabins in Leadville, Colorado were designed as micro dormitories for the Colorado Outward Bound School. The cabins sit lightly on the landscape, elevated above the winter snowpack on steel columns. The client's brief called for 21 cabins, seven senior staff insulated cabins for year-round use, and 14 uninsulated cabins to meet the housing needs during peak season.

In the spring of 2015, the first group of 28 students undertook the 14 uninsulated cabins. They were conceived as two simple elements: a "box" and a "frame". The frame, consisting of three structural steel bays, handles both the gravity and lateral loads of the building. A snow roof of

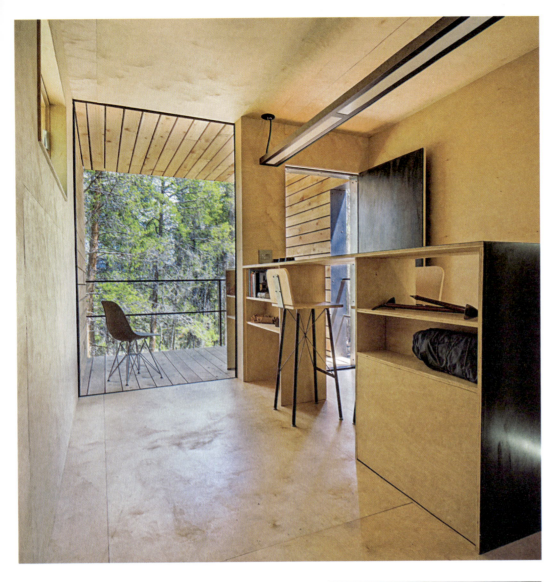

steel N decking, able to span 12' while supporting a 100 PSF snow load, completes the frame. The orientation and articulation of each of the 14 cabins react individually to the immediate site conditions present in the landscape. No two cabins are alike.

In the spring of 2016, the second group of 28 students designed and built seven insulated cabins for year-round use. These structures were required to meet the standards of the International Energy Conservation Code climate zone 7 & 8. Inspired by quinzees, a snow shelter made from a hollowed out pile of snow, the students adapted the logic of "snow insulation" for their structures. The cabins employ structurally insulated panels (SIPs) for the walls and flat roofs. A single electrical circuit powers each structure. This is supported by the small cabin footprints, LED lighting, and the super insulation of the SIPs combined with the snow's natural insulation. This efficiency reflects the school's commitment to the environment.

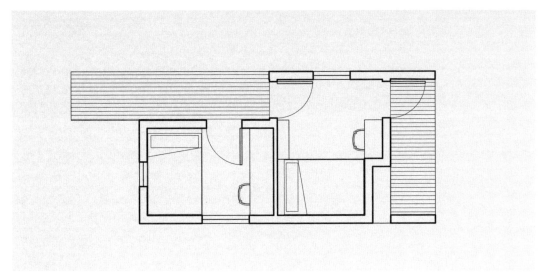

Floor plan – Cabin B

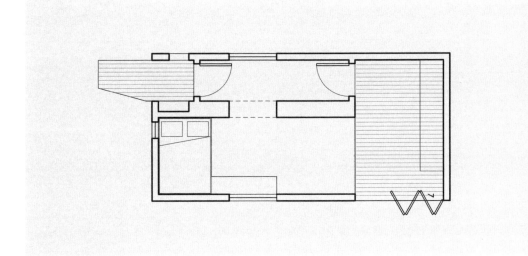

Floor plan – Cabin E

Rooms: 1 bedroom
Main materials: hot rolled steel
and birch plywood
Country of manufacture: USA
Building price: 1,080 $ / sqm
Special design features: custom
structurally insulated panels
for envelope, CNC cabinetry
for interior furniture

NOA Cabin Sõmeru vald, Estonia

Architect: Jaanus Orgusaar/Borealis
Project address: Lepiku talu, Koovälja küla,
Sõmeru vald, Lääne-Virumaa, Estonia
Gross floor area: 21 or 42 sqm
Completion: 2010 and 2014
Photographer: Tõnu Tunnel

NOA Cabin

NOA Cabin

NOA is an easily assembled living unit that fits perfectly into every environment. The modules can be added and rearranged while windows can be transformed into doors at the connecting wall area. While the usual rectangular windows create a frame around a view, the round windows of NOA extend the views. The shape of the house is the result of joining the tips of a cube and icosahedron. It rests on six poles and three corners of the building that reach to the ground. As a result, the building has a comb-shaped floor plan with identically sized trapeze-shaped modules as walls. This structure is simple and economical but at the same time strong. The floor beams are located according to the structure of Flower of Life with the added stability of the triangular system. The outer lining has been treated with ferric oxide, while the roof is made of thermal timber.

NOA offers an extraordinary spatial experience characterized by the sacral nature of its space. In spite of a small floor plan, the height and the unusual shape of the rooms create a sensation of a large and airy space.

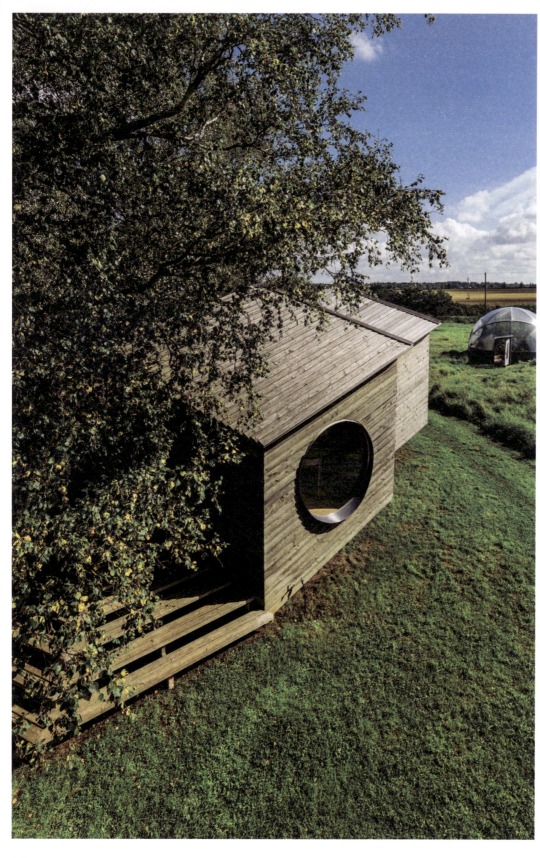

Rooms: kitchen/living area,
1 bedroom and 1 bathroom
Main materials: wood, fur
and lark
Country of manufacture: Estonia
Building price: 5,000 €
Modular extensibility: available

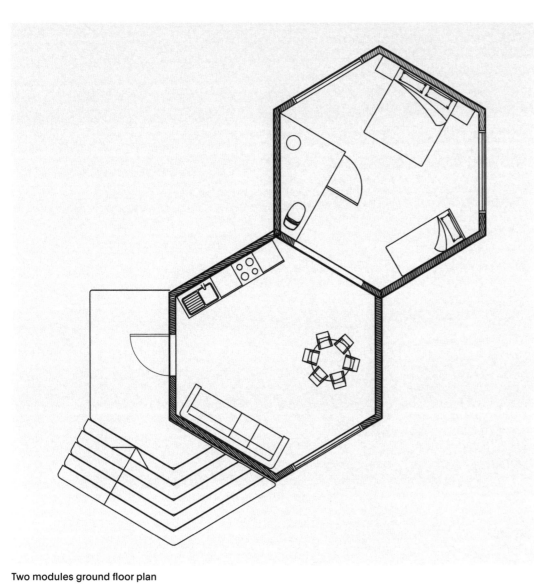

Two modules ground floor plan

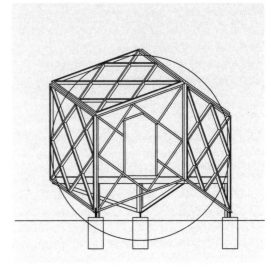

Construction

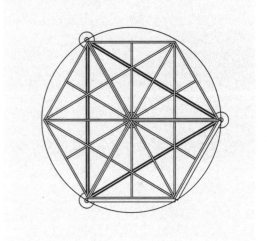

Construction

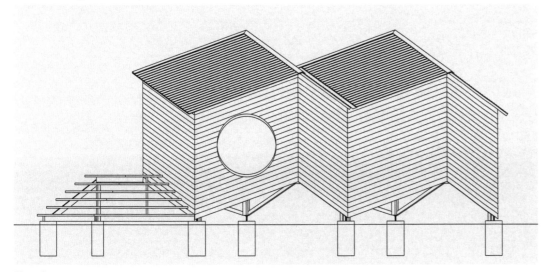

Elevation

Cabin Norderhov, Norway

Architect: Atelier Oslo
Project address: Norderhov, Norway
Gross floor area: 80 sqm
Completion: 2014
Photographer: Lars Petter Pettersen, Atelier Oslo

Cabin Norderhov

Cabin Norderhov

The project is located in Krokskogen forests, outside the town of Hønefoss. Its location on a steep slope gives a fantastic view over the lake Steinsfjorden.

The site is often exposed to strong winds, so the cabin is organized around several outdoors spaces that provide shelter from the wind and allow the sun to enter at different times of the day. The interior is a continuous space. The curved walls and ceilings form continuous surfaces clad with 4mm birch plywood. The floor follows the terrain and divides the plan into several levels that also defines the different functional zones of the cabin.

The transitions between these levels create steps that provide various places for sitting and lying down.

The fireplace is located at the center of the cabin, set down in the floor of the main access level. This provides the feeling of a campfire in the landscape. Seen from all levels in the cabin, you can enjoy the fireplace from far away or lie down next to it.

Outside, the cottage has a rectangular geometry and the walls and roofs are covered with 20 millimeters basalt stone slabs laid in a pattern similar to the ones often used for traditional wooden claddings in Norway.

The lodge consists mainly of prefabricated elements.

The main structure is laminated timber with a substructure of Kerto construction plywood. The Kerto boards are CNC-milled and define both the external and internal geometry. The cabin is supported by steel rods drilled directly into the rock, supplemented with a small concrete foundation under the fireplace for stabilization.

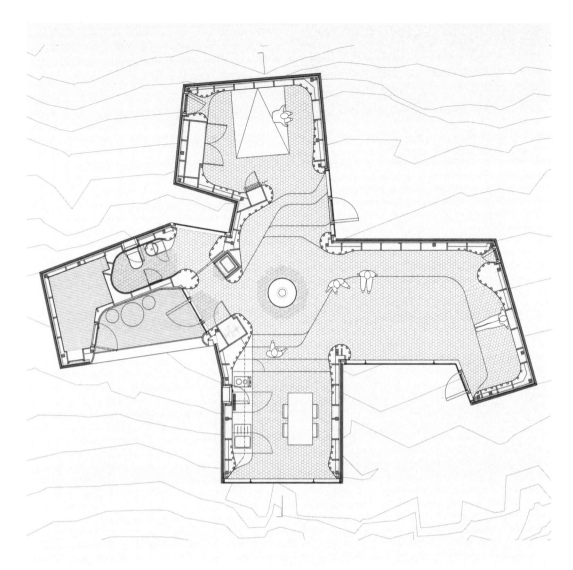

Ground floor plan

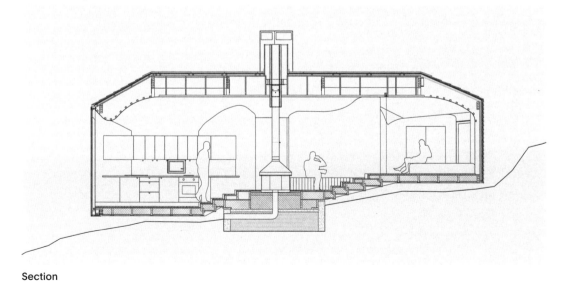

Section

Rooms: kitchen/living area,
1 bedroom and 1 bathrom
Main materials: birch wood,
glass and basalt stone
Country of manufacture: Norway

Treehouse
Riga
Anywhere

Architect: Appleton & Domingos arquitectos
Other creatives involved: JULAR Madeiras
Project address: anywhere
Gross floor area: 47 sqm
Completion: 2010
Photographer: Fernando Guerra – FG+SG

Treehouse Riga

The Treehouse is a prefabricated system of 3.3 × 6.6 m modules that are easily transported in one piece. These can be used to build very large structures according to the buyer's needs and within predefined projects. The houses have the ability to evolve, both during the design phase and after construction, combining housing modules and patio modules.

For reasons of economy and adaptation to different contexts, a language of relatively closed "boxes" was selected in which the openings are well defined and contained.

Based on the Treehouse system, this particular dwelling typology – Riga – was developed as a very compact and flexible structure with only two modules of about 20 square meters each – which aims to meet the demand for limited space housing for both private use and the hotel industry.

Contrary to other Treehouse typologies, this house does not have the capacity to evolve, presenting itself as a closed

project yet highly effective in terms of area utilization. In just two modules of about 20 square meters each, it contains a living room with integrated kitchen and two small bedrooms – one double and the other for children/guests and a shared bathroom.

A birch running wall/door offers great versatility by creating two different houses – one during daytime and another during the night – depending on its position. During the day, the door is positioned to allow the living room to extend to the children/guest room. At night, the running door encloses the children/guest room, ensuring the necessary privacy and allowing independent access from both bedrooms to the bathroom.

Treehouse Riga

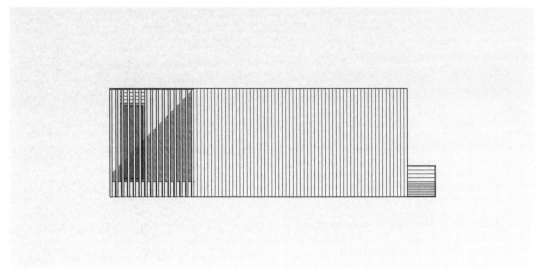

Elevation

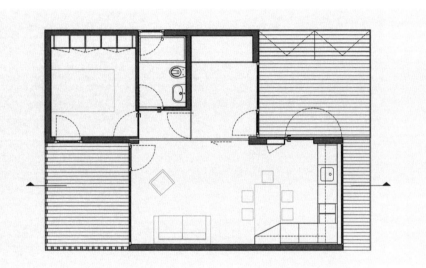

Ground floor plan

Rooms: kitchen/living area,
1+1 bedrooms, and 1 bathroom
Main materials: wood
(LVL structure, larch clapboard
and flooring, gypsum boards,
birch plywood)
Country of manufacture:
Portugal
Building price: 56,000 €

Writers' Cottage 2 Oslo, Norway

Architect: Jarmund/Vigsnæs AS Arkitekter MNAL
Structural engineering: Gunnar Johansson AS
Project address: Oslo, Norway
Gross floor area: 15 sqm
Completion: 2014
Photographer: Jonas Adolfsen

Writers' Cottage 2

This small annex is located in the garden of two professionals in a residential area on the outskirts of the city.

The clients wanted a place that would give them room and quietude to focus on their writing and work. At the same time, they wanted a view that would somehow remind them of their native West-Norwegian landscapes, in spite of the site's location only offering views towards a parking lot and a train station. Their intention was for the project to serve as an alternative to a cottage in the countryside.

The project was located at the edge of a northern slope facing the station, with dense shrubs and weeds below and on either side. To maximize the view, the entire northern façade consists of glass, providing ample natural light for the workspace inside. In order to not obstruct the view, the desk is made completely out of glass. All of this seems to lift

the space above the surrounding landscape.

The project is elevated towards
the south to reach above the
neighbor's hedge and allow
direct sunlight to flow in to the
interior. The plan is also made
narrower towards the south, to
avoid too much sunlight that
could disturb the workplace, as
well as providing privacy from
the garden and the surrounding
houses. The overall shape of the
building is a result of the tran-
sition from the more horizontal
north elevation to the vertical
south elevation.

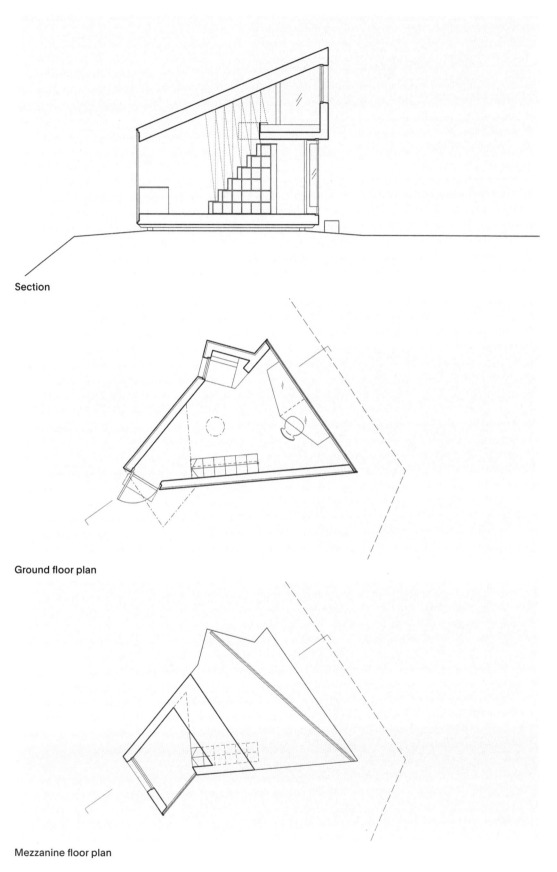

Section

Ground floor plan

Mezzanine floor plan

Rooms: 1 workspace and mezzanine with relaxation area
Main materials: wood
Country of manufacture: Norway

Chameleon Cabin Tjolöholms Slott, Sweden

Architect: White Arkitekter
Printer: Göteborgstryckeriet
Brand agency: Happy F+B
Project address: Tjolöholms Slott, Sweden
Gross floor area: 7 sqm
Completion: 2013
Photographer: Rasmus Norlander

White Arkitekter designed a house made entirely of paper – Chameleon Cabin – that changes appearance like a chameleon depending on the angle from which it is viewed. It shimmers like marble in black and white. Architecture is always perceived in motion and this is what Mattias Lind, lead architect, utilized to create an illusion with Chameleon Cabin. The design concept is based on a corrugated outer surface. A construction that makes the house change color as you move around it and at the same time increases the stability. By printing images of white and black marble on the façade, the architect wants to make a modest everyday material more beautiful. For the interior, a bright yellow was chosen to create a warm feel while contrasting against the discrete black and white of the façade. The house consists of 95 modules and weighs around

100 kilograms. The inner surface is about seven square meters and the house is three meters high. It is built of sheets of Miniwell, corrugated paper that is two millimeters thick, in the format 1,200 × 1,600 millimeters. Compared to other cardboard material, Miniwell is stiffer in relation to its own weight. It consists of a durable material that provides good stability. The roof and façade is suspended with hangers, in a solution similar to Lego, which makes the house easy to assemble and adjust. The design is flexible and can be extended several hundred meters if needed. The result was preceded by numerous full-scale tests in which the house was assembled to ensure stability and develop an interesting architectural form.

Chameleon Cabin

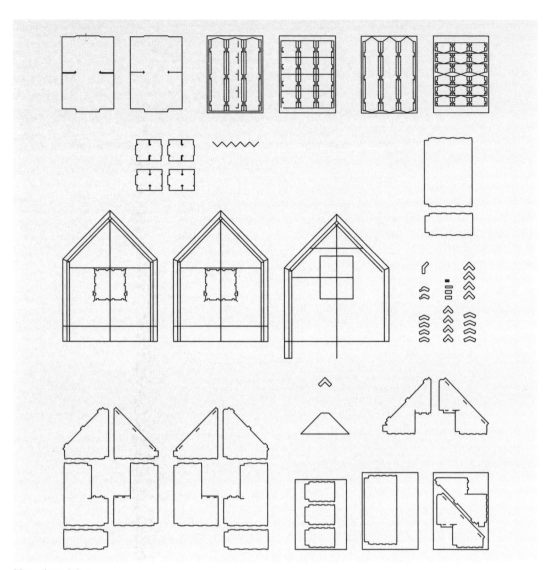

Map of modules

Rooms: 1
Main materials: 2 mm thick
Miniwell corrugated paper
Country of manufacture:
Sweden
Modular extensibility: the
design is flexible and possible
to extend several hundred
meters if needed
Special design features:
entirely made of paper

GOMOS #1 Arouca, Portugal

Architect: SUMMARY – Samuel Gonçalves
Project address: Quinta do Serrado,
Penso, 4540-144 Arouca, Portugal
Gross floor area: 80 sqm
Completion: 2015
Photographer: Tiago Casanova

The Gomos System is based on a business R&D project and consists of a concrete modular system that presents an accurate and efficient answer to the contemporary need to simplify and accelerate building processes. The main idea is derived from the construction system of ordinary sewer pipes, which was re-designed to make it habitable, keeping the characteristics and the stability of canalization shells. It is an evolutionary system, in which each module leaves the factory fully ready. The on-site assembly of the building is completed in a few days, by joining these modules. The building process can be summarized in four phases: structure production, cladding and hardware, transportation and assembly. From a technical

point of view, four key factors led to the development of this project:

Flexibility – The design makes the system flexible, allowing it to be used for different applications besides housing, while accommodating further expansion of the construction.
Ease of transportation – The module was optimized to facilitate transportation, also ensuring dimensions that comply with all applicable legislation.
Energy efficiency – The choices made for the inner layout, including natural ventilation corridors and insulation and lighting, allow obtaining low-energy buildings.
Construction quality – All components are manufactured in factory environments under highly controlled conditions.

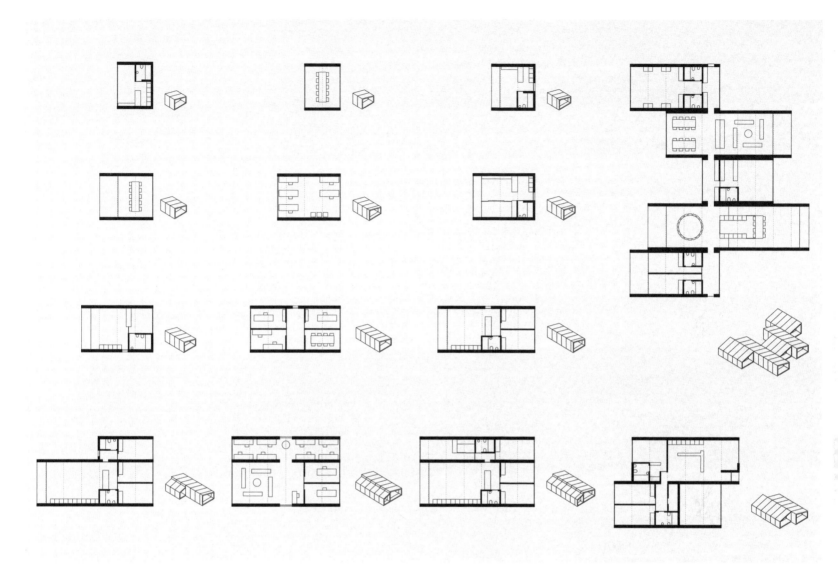

Floor plans and sketches of the extensibility

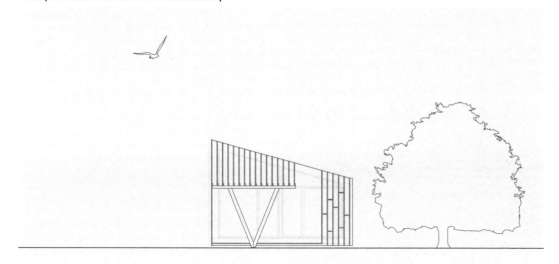

Elevation

Rooms: kitchen/living area, 2 bedrooms and 1 bathroom
Main materials: precast concrete, wood and slate
Country of manufacture: Portugal
Building price: 65,000 €

House Husarö Stockholm, Sweden

Architect: Tham & Videgård Arkitekter
Project address: Österåker,
Stockholm archipelago, Sweden
Gross floor area: 180 sqm
Completion: 2012
Photographer: Ake E:son Lindman

House Husarö

The location is the outer Stockholm archipelago. Tall pines on the forested site give it an untouched character. It stands in a clearing on an elevated plateau overlooking the sea, facing north. The light conditions, the sea view, and the flat and smooth bedrock were some of the qualities that became the initial inspiration for the house. A relatively low budget and the wish to maximize the volume of the building according to the limits set by local building regulations also influenced the design, resulting in the idea to use tectonic rationality to support a specific spatial structure.

The volume of the pitched roof on two levels is divided into an open social area on the ground floor and a more private upper floor for bedrooms and a playroom. Within the square plan, a

freestanding box comprising kitchen, bathroom, and the stairs organizes the ground floor into a sequence of interconnected spaces. Large sliding windows let in sunlight, offering wide views and direct access to the outdoor areas on the naturally flat part of the bedrock. On the upper level, a skylight, running along the ridge of the roof, underscores the verticality of space and subtly enhances the experience of seclusion.

The exterior is entirely clad with folded black sheet metal of varied width. Large sliding doors provide entrances and direct access to the outdoor areas on the naturally flat part of the bedrock. All construction and finishes are made out of wood with sliding doors and windows in hardwood.

House Husarö

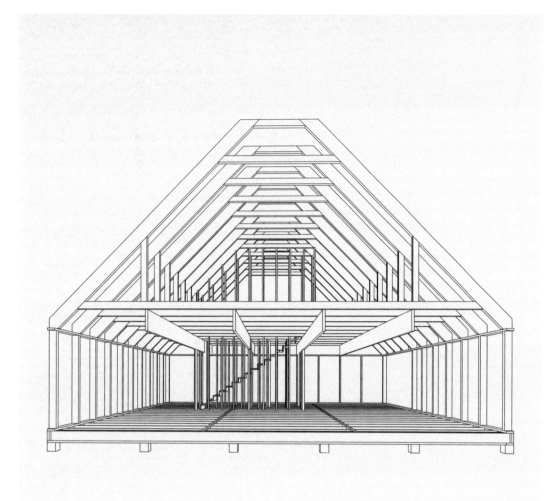

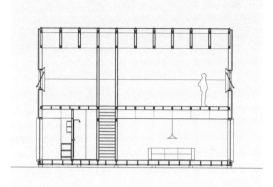

Section

Perspective – Frame structure

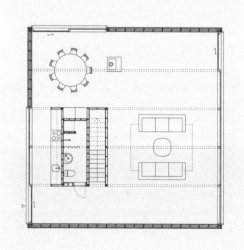

Ground floor plan

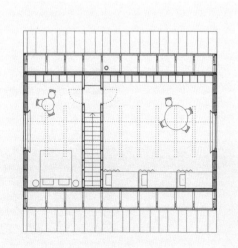

First floor plan

Rooms: kitchen/living area,
2 bedrooms and 1 bathroom
Main materials: wood
Country of manufacture:
Sweden
Building price: 265,000 €

Nido
Sipoo,
Finland

Architect: Robin Falck
Project address: Sipoo, Finland
Gross floor area: 9 sqm
Completion: 2011
Photographer: Robin Falck

Nido

Nido

This cabin was designed by 20-year-old Robin Falck prior to his military service in 2010. It took him two and a half weeks to finish. Nido means "birds nest" in Italian (fitting because Falck is falcon in Swedish).

Located in the beautiful Finnish archipelago of Sipoo with a beautiful view across the sea, the cabin was designed to be built without a permit, measuring just under nine square meters. Robin wanted to maximize the use of this space by focusing on the essentials and stripping away all unnecessary parts, a philosophy Robin now follows as a designer. The cabin contains a lounge/living room with a large window to welcome the beautiful nature, along with plenty of natural light and sufficient storage space.

The top floor has a bed and room for clothes and books. The table and speaker legs were designed and built out of the leftover materials. Robin wanted to maximize the use of materials and minimize waste. He used

local wood and the help of a local carpenter to build the window frame and door. The cabin is isolated with flax and is heated during the winter season with a small heating fan.

Colors and hues were chosen to mimic a large boulder that allowed Nido to easily melt into its surroundings. Everything was carried by hand to the site to damage nature as little as possible during the construction.

As a result, it looks like the cabin has been there for years already.

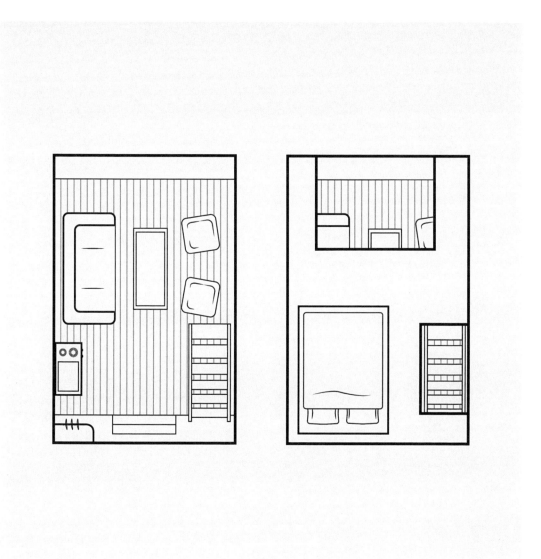

Floor plans

Rooms: kitchen/living area
and 1 bedroom
Main materials: wood,
(spruce & birch)
Country of manufacture: Finland
Building price: 10,000 €

Summer-house T Stockholm, Sweden

Architect: Krupinski/Krupinska Arkitekter
Project address: Stockholm, Sweden
Gross floor area: 40 sqm
Completion: 2015
Photographer: Åke E:son Lindman

Summerhouse T

Summerhouse T

The small house is situated by a lake in the Stockholm archipelago, on a site that was inhabited by a gardener in the early 1900s. Plants and paved walls of that time remain largely in place today. For the last 25 years, another garden-loving family has used the old existing house as a summer home. The family, consisting of mother and two daughters, has grown in recent years when the two daughters established families of their own, which made more space necessary. One sister renovated an existing guesthouse, while the other decided to build a new small house, Summerhouse T, for her family of two adults and two children. The family formulated a program that included a kitchen, bathroom, dining area, living room, four beds and room for storage. While municipal constraints did not allow a building that exceeded 40 sqm.

A large open square room with a standalone volume containing the beds, kitchen, and storage was created. Along the building's southern side are a dining area and a living area. Roof, floor, and walls have a dark color to enhance the building's intimate character and direct the eye towards the surrounding view. The

house's only (trap) door leads to the bathroom, a separate volume, whose design was adapted to fit into an existing gap in the nearby rock.

The open layout with ceiling-high windows creates a large number of different spatial experiences. Freedom of movement along the entire façade gives a feeling that the house is larger and more spacious than it really is. The parents' sleeping area has a view of the countryside and the lake while the children's more enclosed sleeping alcove directs the view towards the grandmother's house. The storage passage at the back of the house opens up to the greenery outside at one end while the parallel kitchen has contrasting views in opposite directions.
The living room with dining area and lounge has a 180-degree-view of its surroundings. Two of the walls are sliding windows that on hot summer days easily open and allow for a pleasant breeze through the house and at the same time extend the living area to the exterior. On rainy days, water runs along the eaves almost as a physically present curtain and the house suddenly closes inward.

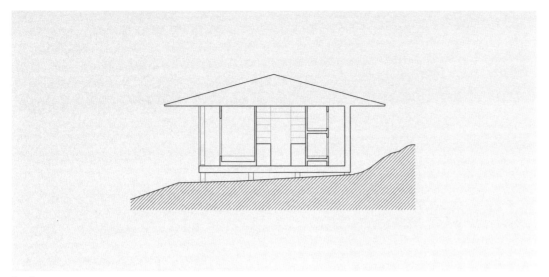

Section

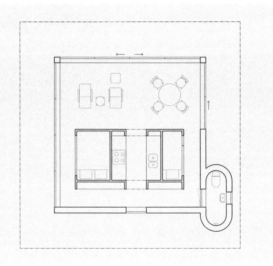

Ground floor plan

Rooms: kitchen/living room,
2 bedrooms and 1 bathroom
Main materials: wood
Country of manufacture:
Sweden

Aggie House Cornwall, United Kingdom

Architect: IPT Architects with Ecospace Studios
Project address: Cornwall, United Kingdom
Gross floor area: 35 sqm
Completion: 2012
Photographer: Andy Spain

Aggie House

The brief for this project was to design a retreat on the rugged Cornish coastline for the clients to escape their busy urban lives. The location is situated within a World Heritage Site and needed to be gentle to its surroundings. The retreat is comprised of a main living space with a mini kitchen, shower room, storage space, and a mezzanine sleeping pad above. With the exception of the floor, the entire interior is finished in birch wood. This includes the kitchen, internal doors, and fitted furniture that all appear as if carved out of a single piece of wood.

The building is cut into the cliff and the roof slope that follows the topography of the site is continued to the interior. Traditional board-on-board timber cladding wraps the entire exterior with the outer layer continuing over some of the glazed areas to address local concerns of light pollution without compromising on the beautiful framed views towards the coastline. This cladding arrangement can also be experienced from the interior.

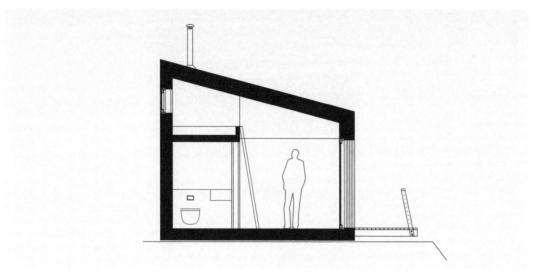

Section

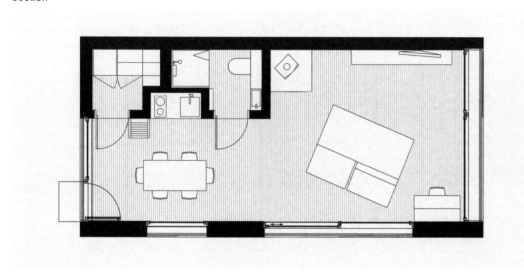

Ground floor plan

Rooms: kitchen/dining/living
area, mezzanine with bed
and 1 bathroom
Main materials: larch, sips
construction, NorDan windows
Country of manufacture:
United Kingdom
Building price: 121,000 £

Delta Shelter Washington, USA

Architect: Olson Kundig
Project address: Mazama, Washington, USA
Gross floor area: 92.9 sqm
Completion: 2002
Photographer: Benjamin Benschneider and
Tim Bies / Olson Kundig

Delta Shelter

Delta Shelter – a 1,000-square-foot (92.9 square meters) cabin – is essentially a steel-clad box on stilts that can be completely shuttered when the owner is away. The 200-square-foot (18.5 square meters) footprint of the house rises above a 40-acre, 100-year flood plain adjacent to the Methow River. The verticality, coloring and raw nature of the materials used for construction directly respond to the wildness of the setting. The owner sought a compact, easy to maintain, virtually indestructible building for himself and his friends for fun and adventure in the mountains. With an exterior of steel, the house is virtually indestructible.

The cabin is composed of three levels: the lowest level is half carport, half utility/storage room; the middle level consists of the entry, two small bedrooms, and bathrooms; and the top level is one large space that includes living, dining, and cooking areas. Cantilevered steel decks extend from the top and middle levels and provide space for outdoor sleeping and entertaining.

The cabin is supported by four steel columns. The floors feature 3-inch by 6-inch tongue-and-groove wood car decking, and the exterior wood infill walls are clad in 16-gauge, hot-rolled steel sheets with exposed steel fasteners. Most of the structure, including the steel structure, roof panels, shutters, and stairs, was prefabricated off-site, thereby reducing on-site waste and site disruption. Due to prefabrication and the use of plywood for all interior surfaces, typical construction wastage was kept to a minimum.

East section

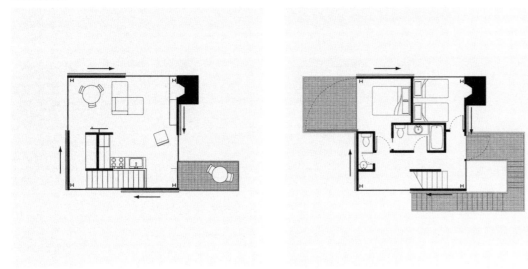

Living level plan

Sleeping level plan

Rooms: kitchen/living/
dining area, 1 bedroom
and 1 bathroom
Main materials: wood and steel
Country of manufacture: USA

standard hOuse Pszczyna, Poland

Architect: Robert Konieczny KWK Promes
Structural engineering: Grzegorz Komraus
Project address: Pszczyna, Poland
Gross floor area: 115 sqm
Completion: 2011
Photographer: Mariusz Czechowicz

standard hOuse

The project evolved under unique conditions: it was supposed to be built in two different places – near Pszczyna and in the outskirts of Berlin. As the second location was still to be chosen, the main goal was to design a house that fits every plot. This is how the idea of standard hOuse emerged, the first attempt of its kind in the history of KWK Promes. The round shape of the house makes it easily suitable to any site shape; the free choice of a roof type makes it universal in terms of environmental conditions, while the flexibility of the interior layout allows it to be matched to the needs of individual families.

Sustainability is the focal point of the design of the house: it was designed to respect the environment by choosing natural building materials and using renewable energy sources. The use of prefabricated wooden construction allowed reduction of the building costs coupled with good quality. Owing to the building's optimal shape (circle), very good thermal insulation, elimination of thermal bridges, and renewable energy installations the house can be classified as passive.

standard hOuse

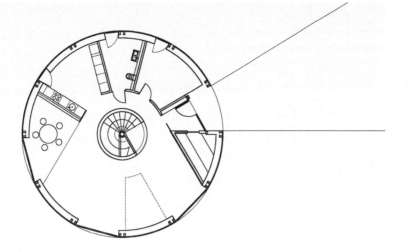

Ground floor plan

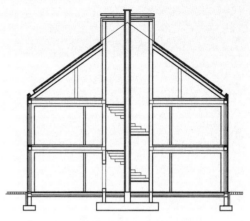

Section

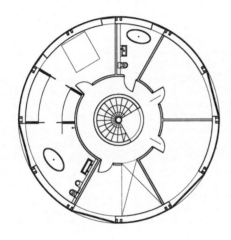

First floor plan

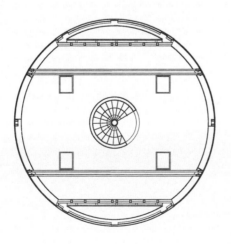

Second floor plan

Rooms: kitchen/living/dining area, 4 bedrooms and 3 bathrooms
Main materials: prefabricated wood
Country of manufacture: Poland

VIMOB
Rozo,
Colombia

Architect: COLECTIVO CREATIVO arquitectos
Project address: Matapalo, Palmira,
Valle del Cauca, Colombia
Gross floor area: 37.02 sqm
Completion: 2015
Photographer: Felipe Orvi and
Mauricio Carvajal

VIMOB was born from the notion of creating a shelter in an area of difficult access, a place where building a traditional construction would be limited by transport of materials and labor. It is a modular solution, based on the concept of prefabrication and assembly, capable of offering the essential space of a traditional construction in a practical, flexible, attractive, and modern prototype. It is structured from carefully studied modules, articulated with harmony and sobriety in a cozy atmosphere, allowing the enjoyment of the environment and providing an image of high standing. VIMOB was developed in a workshop, dismantled, and sent to the construction site directly. The modules allowed fast assembly on site, using a mini-

mum of tools. Each component of the project was designed to be adapted and adjusted to the module frame, thus reducing on-site finishing and labor, minimizing the waste of raw materials, carbon footprint, and impact on natural and unforeseen events. This archetype of clean, simple lines aims to be meticulous in its details and modulation, architects differentiate the

materials and textures with hues of earth colors. In the interior, wood predominates on walls, the OSB panel and pine ceilings. In the lounge area, transparency is achieved by openings, with large sliding glass doors that provide easy access to the front terrace, for a permanent relationship between the exterior and interior and an interesting effect of light and contrasts.

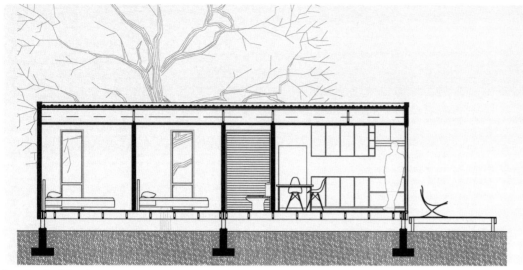

Longitudinal Section

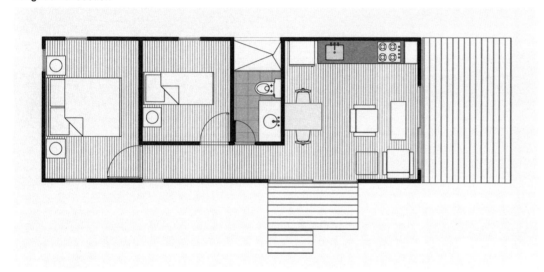

Ground floor plan

Rooms: kitchen/living area,
2 bedrooms and 1 bathroom
Main materials: steel, OSB,
fibercement plate and
laminated wood
Country of manufacture:
Colombia
Building price: 22,824 $
Modular extensibility: 11-15-0001

Island House Breukelen, The Netherlands

Architect: 2by4-architects
Project address: Breukelen, The Netherlands
Gross floor area: 21 sqm
Completion: 2011
Photographer: 2by4-architects

On an island of 5 by 100 meters in the Dutch lake area, "Loosdrechtse Plas" 2by4-architects designed a unique recreational house. The house acts as a subtle frame that captures the view from the inside-out and outside-in. 2by4 designed the house in such a way that it can customize the interaction with the surrounding nature. One of the glass façade can be completely opened so that the wooden outdoor terrace becomes part of the interior. To lift the inside-outside barrier even more, the dark wooden façade can be folded open, creating a panoramic view of nature. The folded façade becomes an abstract perpendicular element that floats above the water. By opening this part of the façade, the wooden floor of the living area is now directly connected to the water allowing inhabitants to access the lake from the living room.

Although the size of the house is limited, it still contains all the functions that are needed for comfort. Shower, toilet, kitchen, closets, storage, and other functions are all integrated into a double wall. According to the need of a specific function the wall can be modified so that the spatial configuration

Island House

changes, resulting in different atmospheres. The fireplace also contributes to the changing of atmospheres because it can be rotated towards the outdoor terrace for cozy summer evenings.

Visitors that arrive at the house enter it in a series of sequences. Seen from the mainland, the house floats above the island.

Arriving on the island itself, the visitors are guided towards an elevated jetty that brings them to the terrace on the other side. The terrace continues towards the inside of the house where it stops halfway. Here the floor changes material and becomes a raised platform from where the visitors can look back at the nature they just came from.

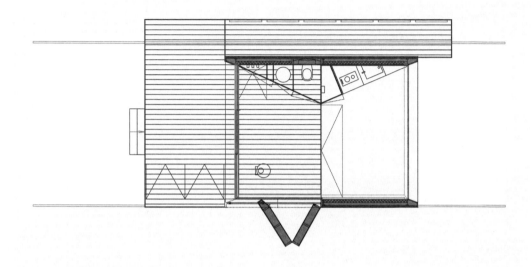

Ground floor plan

Rooms: kitchen/living/
sleeping area and 1 bathroom
Main materials: steel, wood
and glass
Country of manufacture:
The Netherlands
Modular extensibility: available
Special design features: façade
can be folded open

Mono-View Cottage Østfold, Norway

Architect: Reiulf Ramstad Arkitekter
Project address: Fuglevik, Østfold, Norway
Gross floor area: 130 sqm
Completion: 2011
Photographer: Reiulf Ramstad Arkitekter

Mono-View Cottage

This summer retreat is designed around the concept of a mono-view, meaning that the house opens up to the landscape in one direction only. The stunning views of the Oslofjord are framed by its fully glazed walls towards the sea, while it is almost entirely opaque from the back.

The simple rectangular volume is clad with untreated cedar wood, providing a clean-cut expression while emphasizing the building's mass and timber structure. Observing the cottage from a distance gives the impression that it is placed directly onto the ground, not obstructing views from adjacent sites. A solitary frosted window reveals the translucency of the opposite side, its spectacular views implied by a narrow opening between the main body and the annex.

The interior is a continuation of its pure expression, lined in white stained timber without window trims or moldings. The duality of openness gives the entire indoor experience a sense of unambiguous orientation and intensifies the sense of bringing the landscape into the house. It provides a contemplative space to observe the changes of weather and seasons.

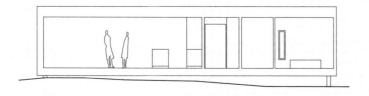

Section

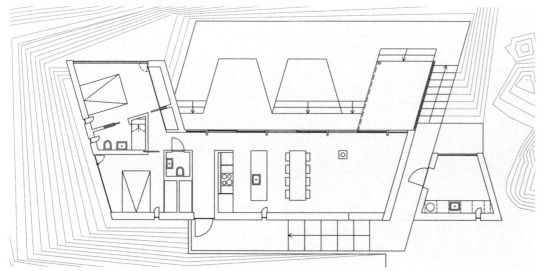

Ground floor plan

Rooms: kitchen/dining/
living area, 2 bedrooms
and 2 bathrooms
Main materials: untreated
cedar wood
Country of manufacture: Norway

Casa
Invisibile
Slovenia

Architect: Delugan Meissl Associated Architects
Project address: Slovenia
Gross floor area: 50 sqm
Completion: 2013
Photographer: www.christianbrandstaetter.com
and Delugan Meissl Associated Architects

Casa Invisibile

Casa Invisibile

Casa Invisibile is a flexible housing unit, which consists of a prefabricated wood structure designed for turnkey implementation at any designated site.

Maximum flexibility and spatial quality are the key elements in its concept of development. The open layout is structured by a chimney and a wet cell, resulting in three spatial units that allow individual use and design. The structure and ambience of the rooms are characterized by the use of domestic woods. The mounting framework and fitments of the housing unit are exclusively assembled from prefabricated elements at the factory. The overall dimensions are 14.50 × 3.50 meters, which allows easy transportation by trucks.

The clients can choose designs and textures for the interior and façade from various options listed in a design catalogue.

This offers tailor-made design options for the housing units coupled with flexible pricing options. Through modular element construction and the intensive use of wood, the housing units can be completely disassembled, thus minimizing their environmental footprint.

By combining innovation and mobility at a reasonable price, Casa Invisibile is a product that offers a ground breaking alternative in an increasingly critical housing situation. Key factors in this unique proposition are its uncomplicated assembly, its attractive price, and the free choice of location. These are considerable advantages of Casa Invisibile compared to the cost-intensive and bureaucratic construction of a conventional house.

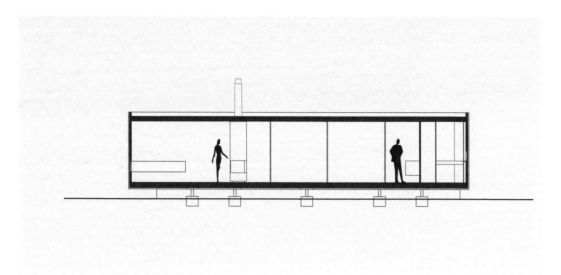

Longitudinal section

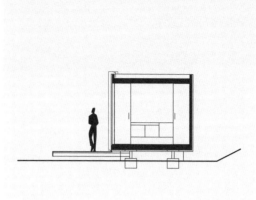

Cross section

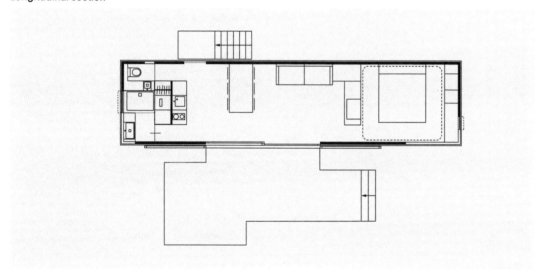

Ground floor plan

**Rooms: kitchen/dining/
living area, 1 bedroom,
1 bathroom and 1 toilet
Main materials: wood,
aluminum and glass
Country of manufacture: Austria
Special design features:
available in three different sizes**

197

Heijmans ONE multiple locations, The Netherlands

Architect: Moodbuilders
Project address: multiple locations, The Netherlands
Gross floor area: 45 sqm
Completion: 2016
Photographer: Arnold Rijndorpand Heijmans

Heijmans ONE

The aim of this project was to design a house whose residents would be proud to live in. Not a container, but a normal dwelling with the added value of transportability. The dwelling connects sustainable wood architecture with recognizable Dutch housing iconography. The asymmetric roof creates a variation effect when multiple houses come together.

The context of the Heijmans ONE: It is almost impossible to find good and affordable accommodation for fresh graduates who recently started their first job. They earn a bit too much to qualify for social rental programs, or there are too many others in the same situation. At the same time, renting in the open sector is too expensive because they still want to enjoy life in their spare time. Buying is also expensive, and is not really a viable option in this phase of their lives. Therefore, it is about time some attention was given to this group!

"Can we create a house which appeals to today's young generation?" was the ultimate design challenge of Heijmans ONE, which stands for affordability and comfort. The concept allows tenants to rent a complete house for around 700/ 800 € per month; a house with character and its own appeal. The intelligent layout, with a lot of natural light, a mezzanine, and decorative wood finish makes the 45 square meters feel large and spacious. In addition, it also offers a private patio and the house can be furbished in accordance with the residents' lifestyle.

Section

Ground floor plan

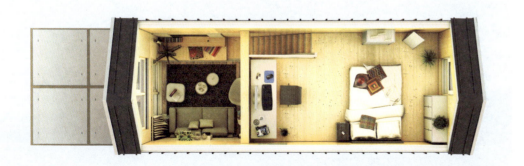

First floor plan

Rooms: kitchen/living area, 1 bedroom and 1 bathroom
Main materials: cross laminated timber
Country of manufacture: The Netherlands
Building price: 64,500–72,500 €
Modular extensibility: variation in roof shapes and top configuration

MINIMOD Catuçaba São Paulo, Brazil

Architect: MAPA Architects
Project address: Fazenda Catuçaba,
São Paulo, Brazil
Gross floor area: 42 sqm (each unit)
Completion: 2015
Photographer: Leonardo Finotti

MINIMOD Catuçaba

MINIMOD Catuçaba is a primitive retreat with a contemporary reinterpretation, which aims to offer a remote-landscape experience. MINIMOD presents an alternative to traditional construction: based on prefabricated plug&play logics, it incorporates the benefits that new technology has to offer. Quiet but not shy, it is unique in Brazil due to the use of CLT

Wood Technology, which combines the efficiency of industrialized products with the sustainability of new technologies and the sensitivity of the par excellence natural material.

MINIMOD exploration started in 2009 and still goes on. The first prototype was constructed in Porto Alegre and installed near a lake in the southern wild

landscapes. Since then a number of new locations have been explored. Both projects presented here belong to a new MINIMOD generation, which enriches the idyllic Fazenda Catuçaba.

This old Fazenda is located in the east of SãoPaulo Estate surrounded by a chain of coastal mountains. Catuçaba's MINIMODs move away from the old central house and seek the perfect terrain. On top of a hill, on the edge of a small pond, near a stream, or on the bottom of a valley – each adapts to its new landscape to empower it.

Both MINIMOD Catuçabas were built in a factory in an industrial town near São Paulo. They were transported in modules for over 150 km, before being installed on site with the help of crane trucks. Geographically, these two first MINIMOD Catuçaba units are located in different places 1,000 meters away from each other. They adopt different spatial configurations as a response to each situation.

Ground floor plan (X shape unit)

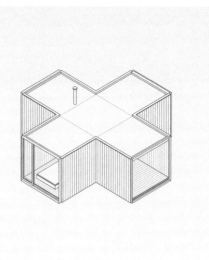

Isometric view (X shape unit)

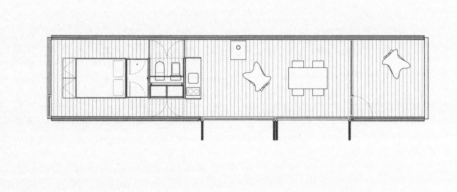

Ground floor plan (I shape unit)

Isometric view (I shape unit)

**Rooms: kitchen/dining area,
2 bedrooms (X shape unit),
1 bedroom (I shape unit) and
1 bathroom
Main materials: wood and cross
laminated timber (CLT)
Country of manufacture: Brazil**

Tom's Hütte Wienerwald, Austria

Architect: raumhochrosen – Heike Schlauch and Robert Fabach
Project address: Wienerwald, Austria
Gross floor area: 28.5 sqm
Completion: 2012
Photographer: Albrecht Imanuel Schnabel

Tom's Hütte

The shelter is situated at the edge of the forest in a peripheral area of the Vienna Woods. The next village is a few kilometers away. A meadow, a forested slope, leaves on the ground, rocks jutting out of the ground in some areas, a northern slope on which the snow does not melt for a long time in spring and is wonderfully cool in summer – all of this constitutes the ideal retreat from the noisy city with all its sensory overload for the owner, an Austrian song writer and coach. The simple house strongly reflects its surroundings, following the outline of its predecessor whose shape seemed to have been interwoven with the location. This is why it became the base for retelling the story of a forest hut in this location with small additions. The building was

literally designed around the person and his passions. An angular structure encases the living area of this shelter on two levels. Totally closed with only one opening on each side, the hut can be opened for various views. Prefabricated from wood, all necessities of life are found in its confined space. There is an indoor and an outdoor fireplace and water is provided by a spring on the lot. There is no electricity and only a simple stove for cooking and heating. The folding shutter on the window at the same time serves as a bench. The untreated wood naturally incorporates the dwelling into its natural surroundings, offering protection, rest, inner peace, and equilibrium.

Tom's Hütte

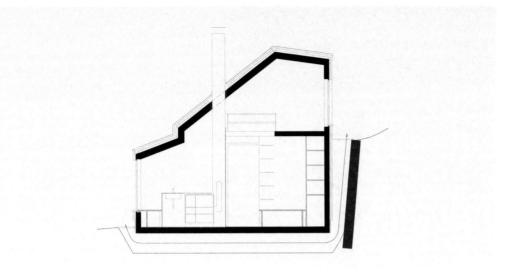

Section

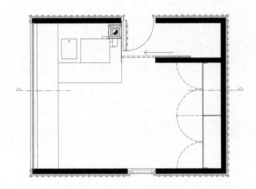

Ground floor plan

**Rooms: kitchen/living area,
mezzanine with bed
Main materials: wood
Country of manufacture: Austria**

Home in Rodersdorf, Switzerland

Architect: Berrel Berrel Kräutler Architekten
Project address: Landskronstrasse, 4118 Rodersdorf, Switzerland
Gross floor area: 172.05 sqm
Completion: 2016
Photographer: Eik Frenzel

Home in Rodersdorf

The prefabricated timber house is located on a slope with views across the hills of the Alsace region. The cubature of the single-family home reflects the clever compliance with the building regulation requirements, while the interior is divided into split-levels in such a way that four independent living areas are created. The roof and adjacent façades are covered in a copper titanium-zinc skin, while the long sides are covered in light laths. The materials of the façades emphasize the unique volumes of the timber house.

The house structure is determined by a wooden interior shell that is suspended from the roof and contains the upper floors. The oversized space between the shell and the skin is the highlight of the house and its center

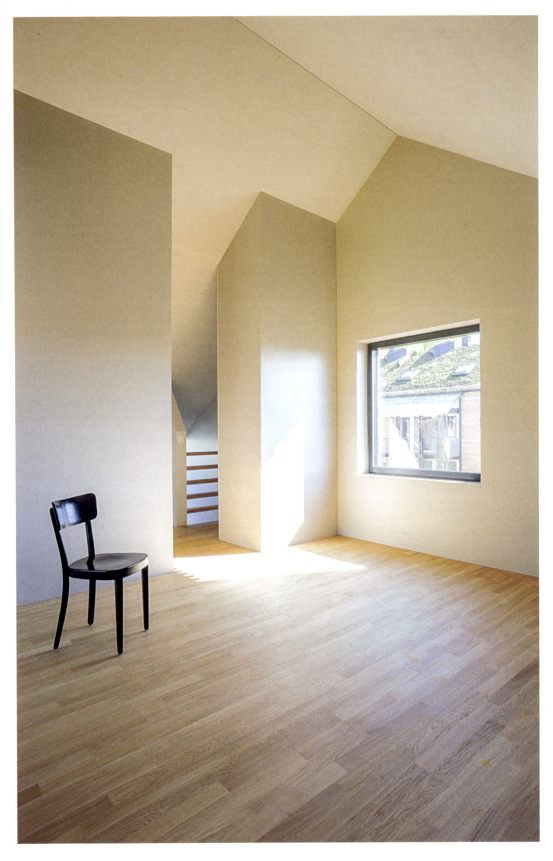

at the same time. It is connected to the exterior spaces via a large window. Small transom light slots in the roof and along the suspended shell allow light to enter the sculptured interior. Its core consists of a wooden fitted piece of furniture that divides and connects the entrance, coat rack, kitchen, dining area, living room, and lounge. The precise carpentry allows these uses to disappear inside the abstract sculpture. The upper floors inside the suspended shell are accesses via minimalist stairways with fitted solid timber stairs. The bedroom, office, and bathroom are separated by fitted closets. Walls and doors are aligned in a straight line without projections.

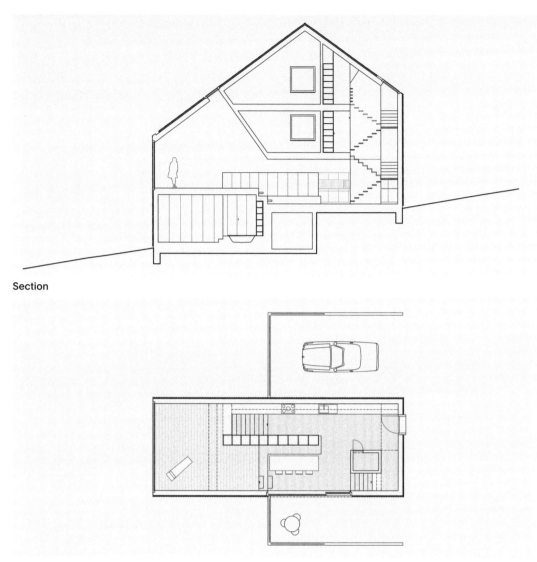

Section

Ground floor plan

Rooms: kitchen/living/dining area, office with library, 1 bedroom, 2 bathrooms, cellar and storerooms
Main materials: wood (supporting structure, façades (long sides), carpentry, floors), metal (façade), concrete (plinth)
Country of manufacture: Switzerland
Building price: 855,000 CHF

Ark-Shelter Anywhere

Architect: Michiel De Backer, Martin Mikovčák
Project address: anywhere
Gross floor area: 27 sqm
Completion: 2015
Photographer: Thomas Debruyne

Ark-Shelter

A group of architectural students came together to reinvent the way people live their lives. In today's fast-paced world, people experience a continuous loop of pressures and deadlines that leave them stressed and burdened. The students found a way to help people escape from this stressed life and return to their roots. They believe that by incorporating nature back into their lives, people will find the break they need.

This is how ARK was born. Based on an appreciation of low-tech architecture, the team created an affordable home that everyone can enjoy. It is essentially

a cocoon without TV, a silent place to reconnect with and appreciate nature, a cozy home where residents can connect with themselves. The philosophy behind ARK is to go back to the basics by proving a living place within nature. With sides that fold open, ARK adjusts to the landscape and becomes an extension of it. Its panoramic views allow the residents to enjoy camping without giving up comfort, unlike anything before. The associated furniture is uniquely designed and crafted from the same wood as the walls, floor, and ceiling, creating a warm and cozy atmosphere. Simple elegance is highly valued.

ARK's mobile and zero impact design allows its owners to change locations while leaving nature untouched. The minimalist design blends with the landscape, letting them enjoy nature by becoming part of it. If they choose to close the shelter from the outside, the natural lights will continue to play an inspiring role inside.

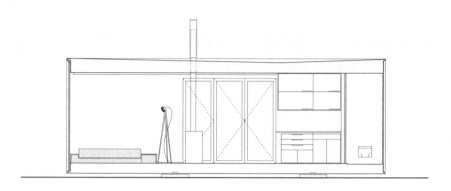

Section

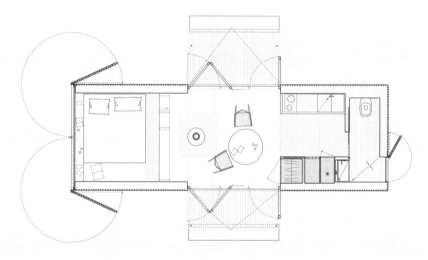

Ground floor plan

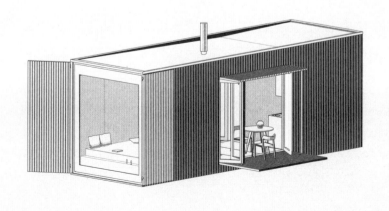

Axonometric projection

Rooms: kitchen/living area,
1 sleeping area and 1 bathroom
Main materials: timber skeleton,
pinetree bioplates, inside oak
floor, façade pinetree coated in
black oil color
Country of manufacture: Slovakia
Building price: 50,000 €
Special design features:
Ark-Shelter can also be off-grid
with solar panels and batteries

The Spinney House Surbiton, United Kingdom

Architect: Ecospace Studios
Project address: Surbiton, United Kingdom
Gross floor area: 50 sqm
Completion: 2016
Photographer: Ben Benoliel

Ecospace Studios specializes in flexible modular buildings that can be simply tailored, reconfigured, or extended, and applied to a diverse range of uses and building types. This project consisted of developing a high-quality sustainable building at a fixed cost and within a short delivery period by combining design and off-site in-house construction. Clad in planks of cedar wood, this partly prefabricated garden hideaway in suburban London is used as a guesthouse as well as a home office. The 50 sqm space created in Surbiton is situated at the bottom of the garden and accommodates a bedroom, kitchen, a living area, and an office space that allows the clients to work from home and host guests. The sloping roof creates a mezzanine above the

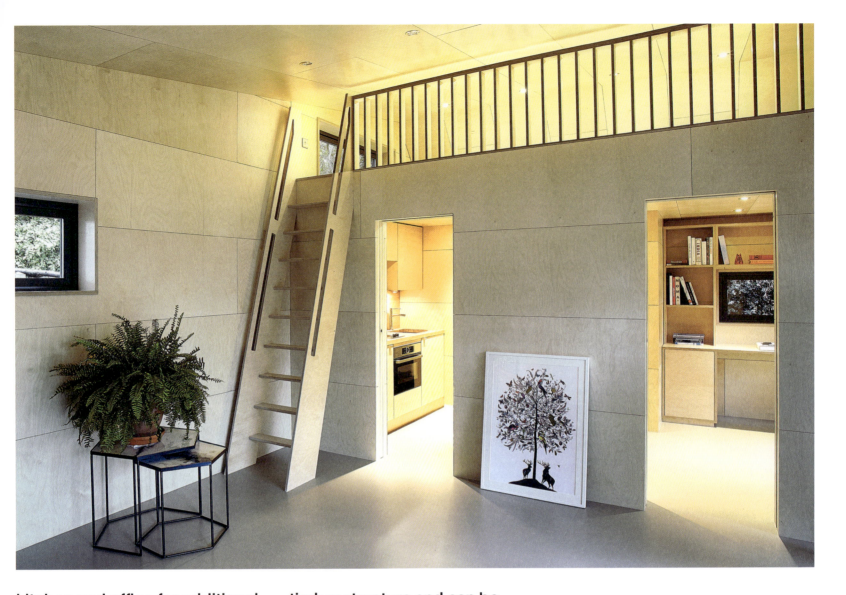

kitchen and office for additional living/sleeping space. Sustainable natural materials were used in an innovative manner including birch wood panels incorporating built-in furniture that wrap the interior. A recyclable rubber floor runs throughout to create a uniform appearance for the open-plan space. A raised decking area stretches across the front of the timber structure and can be accessed via sliding glazing from the living space and bedroom. Ecospace Studios has adapted its modular system to create an extensive portfolio of holiday retreats, compact dwellings and bespoke studios. The prefabricated buildings can be assembled in as little as five days and have a life expectancy of up to 60 years.

The Spinney House

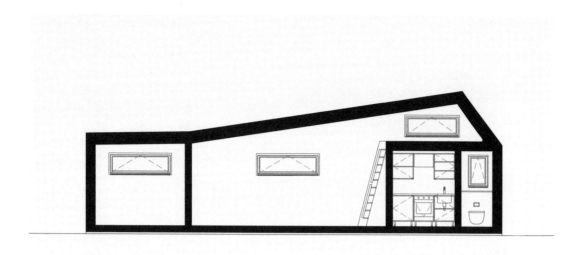

Section

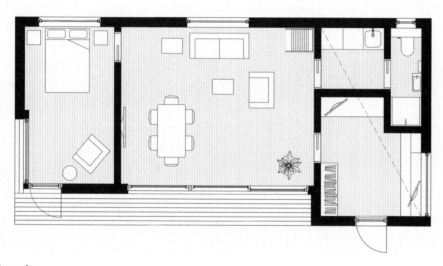

Ground floor plan

Rooms: kitchen/living area,
1 office space, 1 bedroom
and 1 bathroom
Main materials: western red
cedar, sips construction
Country of manufacture:
United Kingdom
Building price: 120,000 £

Moose Road California, USA

Architect: Mork Ulnes Architects
Structural engineer: Double-D Engineering
Project address: Ukiah, CA 95482, USA
Gross floor area: 111 sqm
Completion: 2013
Photographer: Bruce Damonte

Moose Road

Moose Road

Three locally known land formations can be seen from the site: "Eagle Rock," "Goat Rock," and the valley of vineyards below. The main challenge was to frame these three views while preserving existing oak trees on site. In the end, a form with three fingers was designed to extend precise-ly in-between the existing trees, each oriented toward one of the three views.

As a conventional poured foundation would sever the existing tree roots, killing the oaks, an arborist and surveyor helped in locating precise points in

between the roots to anchor piers to the bedrock. The house was then constructed on stilts that sleeved into drilled concrete piers.

At the intersection of the three views, an area was identified between the roots where a tiny foundation could be poured, which stabilized the structure and was the one place where the body of the building touched

the ground. This small concrete foundation supports both a stairway to enter the building and a communal concrete tub – embedded in the floor – with views of the vineyards below. To cut cost as well as meet the sustainability goals of the clients, the building was dimensioned using standard-sized, off-the-shelf sheet goods (unfinished plywood and OSB) to minimize waste, while the interior was finished in those same sheet goods. The building's exterior is clad in thin steel panels that ripple subtly when in the heat of the sun.

Moose Road

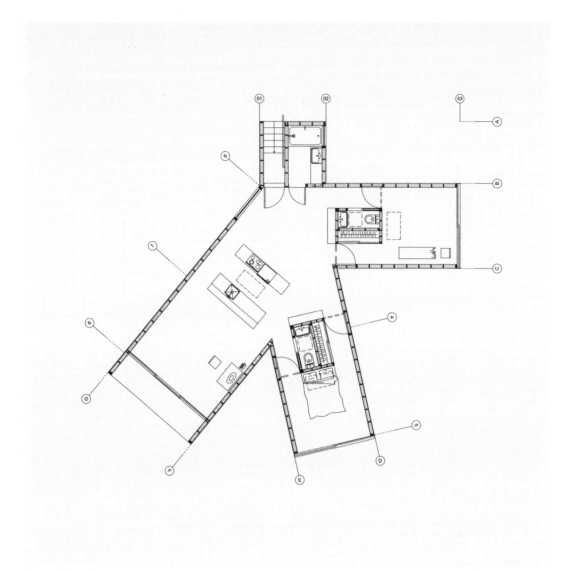

Ground floor plan

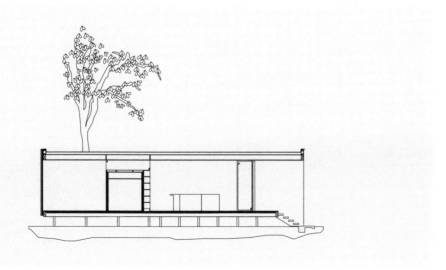

Longitudinal section

Rooms: kitchen/living area, 2 bedrooms and 3 bathroms
Main materials: sealed OSB floors, lye treated plywood walls, ptd. steel & wood structure, ReziBond-coated flat metal siding
Country of manufacture: USA
Building price: $170/sqft

JP House
Cuenca,
Spain

Architect: MYCC Architecture Office
Project address: Tragacete, Cuenca, Spain
Gross floor area: 144 sqm
Completion: 2012
Photographer: Fernando Guerra – FG+SG and
MYCC Architecture Office

JP House

This commission was for a second home in a remote village. The client chose a prefabricated process because the house he wanted could not be built by local traditional constructors. He wanted something different from the traditional houses in the area and, above all, a reliable process. Nevertheless, the house should fit in with the local compact urbanism of the small town. The first sketches already show a compact simple volume and a scale that fits the surroundings. There is also a kind of contemporary action for a house, which will be used just weekends and holidays by an urban family.

The site is on an upper part of the village, oriented to the south

and offering views over the houses to the east. It is big enough for the 144 square meters to be build, and even some free space for a terrace and relaxed outdoor living. Just eight modules of 18 square meters (six times three) and a small piece for the high part were needed. It is based on a simple diagram and every module has its own function. The ground floor holds a master bedroom and a bathroom, the functional module of stairs, facilities and laundry, and a living/dining/kitchen area.

Upstairs there are two bedrooms at the ends, again the functional module of stairs and bathroom, and the elevated room with no clearly defined use. The image of the house is completed by large square holes, facing south and east. The structure is clad in a larch rain screen façade. To reinforce the holiday open living concept, two sliding doors will always be open to the outdoor terrace, made of wood polymer composite.

JP House

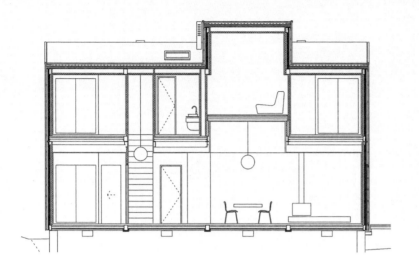

Section

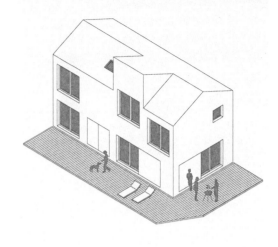

Isometric view

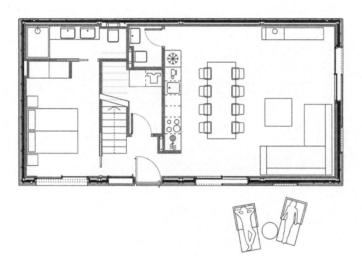

Ground floor plan

Rooms: kitchen/dining/living area, 3 bedrooms, 2 bathrooms and 1 toilet
Main materials: steel and wood
Country of manufacture: Spain
Building price: 146,000 €

MIMA House Comporta, Portugal

Architect: MIMA Architects
Project address: Comporta, Portugal
Gross floor area: 36 sqm
Completion: 2011
Photographer: José Campos

The house has a square plan with nearly identical façades on its four sides. Corner posts support the roof allowing the intervening walls to be fully glazed. The exterior styling is unabashedly modern with clean lines and crisply folded edges.

The 36 sqm (387.5 ftq) interior floor area is divided into a 1.5 meters (4'11'') grid by integrated tracks in the floor and ceiling.

The interior wall system consists of frames that are snapped into place in the tracks. As a result, the rooms can be expanded or reduced in increments of 1.5 meters. Panels are then attached to both sides of the wall frames. These panels are available in a variety of colors or wood veneer.

They can have different colors on either side, so the decor of the house can be changed by simply flipping the panels over. Similar panels can be used to cover the windows if needed for privacy or to block out unwanted sunlight and views.

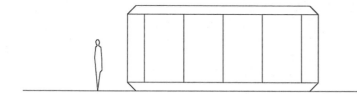

Elevation

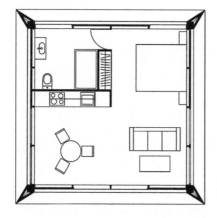

Ground floor plan

Rooms: kitchen/living/ sleeping area, 1 bathroom
Main materials: oak wood, plaster, and white tiles
Country of manufacture: Portugal

Alpine Shelter Skuta, Slovenia

Architect: OFIS architects and AKT II
Other creatives involved: students at Harvard
University Graduate School of Design, Rieder
and Rockwool
Project address: Mountain Skuta, Slovenia
Gross floor area: 12 sqm
Completion: 2016
Photographer: Andrej Gregoric, Janez Martincic

Alpine Shelter Skuta

The project developed from an architectural design studio at the Harvard Graduate School of Design led by Rok Oman and Spela Videcnik from OFIS. In fall 2014, studios of 13 students were facing the challenges of designing an innovative yet practical shelter to meet the needs of the extreme alpine climate. Inspired by the vernacular architecture of Slovenia with its rich and diverse architectural heritage, the students produced 12 proposals meeting various site conditions, material considerations, and programmatic concerns that were produced and catalogued.

The bivouac is an object that represents a basic human necessity, a shelter. It is a symbol of refuge. The outer form and materials were chosen to respond the extreme mountain conditions, and provide views of the greater landscape. Its position within the wilderness requires respect for natural resources, therefore it must meet the ground in a light and firm manner to ensure the shelter is strongly anchored

while having a minimal impact on the ground. The design of the interior is modest and completely subordinated to the function of the shelter providing accommodation for up to eight mountaineers.

The design consists of three modules, in part to allow for transport and to programmati-cally divide the space. The first is dedicated to the entrance, storage and a small space for the preparation of food. The second one provides space for both sleeping and socializing while the third features a bunk sleeping area. Windows at both ends offer beautiful panoramic views of the valley and Skuta Mountain.

Alpine Shelter Skuta

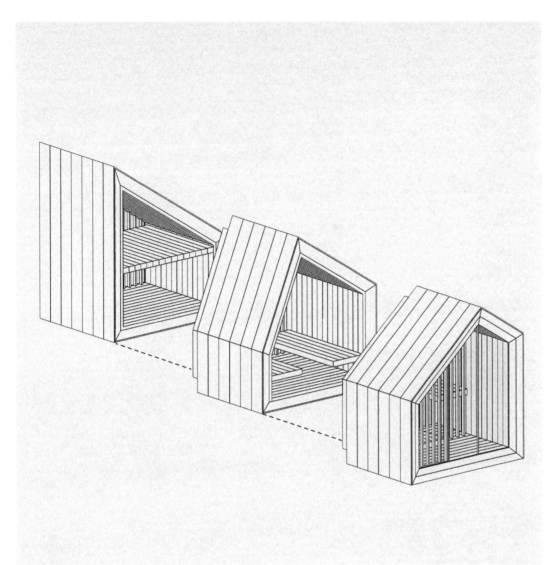

Exploded view

Cross section

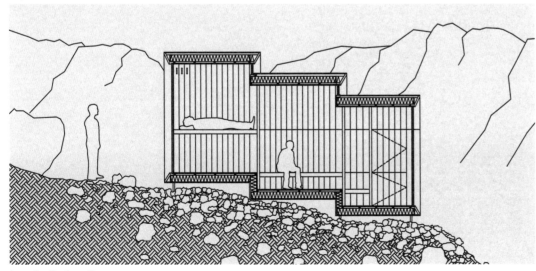

Longitudinal section

Rooms: 1 room with
8 sleeping places
Main materials: Rieder thin glass
fibre öko skin concrete elements
and larch timber in the interior
Country of manufacture:
Slovenia

Exbury Egg Bealieu River, United Kingdom

Architects: PAD studio
Artist: Stephen Turner
Client: Spud Group
Project address: Bealieu River, United Kingdom
Completion: 2013
Photos: Nigel Rigden

Idyllically located on the Exbury bank of the Bealieu River, the Egg is a project for a temporary live/work space for an artist that New Forest-based architectural practice PAD studio developed in partnership with Spudgroup. The project was conceived to bring together architects, artists, and engineers to collaborate on exploring new models for rural architecture, through a series of temporary buildings in the New Forest National Park. The buildings will be a resource for interaction and debate on issues of sustainability, recycling, energy conservation, and rural development, with the artists' residence and activity as the catalyst.

The architect's brief was challenging – the structure had to be sustainable, made of local materials, make minimum intrusion in the landscape and become an artwork itself, as well as a temporary live/work structure. A key aim of the project was also to demonstrate how the arts could engage with environmental issues to generate new perspectives.

Working with renowned artist Stephen Turner, PAD studio identified the unusual site in an exploration up the Beaulieu River.

A fabricated embankment that is effectively an isolated one and a half kilometers long island accessible only by boat at high water or by the very intrepid at low water.

Inspired by birds that lay their eggs along the edge of the river, the Egg will be built by a local boat builder as a cold-molded plywood sheathed timber framed structure with reclaimed timber cladding approximately six meters long and around three meters diameter. The structure will tread lightly upon the site – without direct fixing to the land or river. Strong points built into the Egg's hull enable the Egg to be tethered to points on the land, securing it from lateral movement, but allowing it to rise and fall in line with the tide.

Exbury Egg

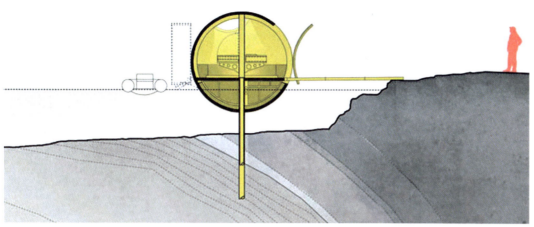

Cross section

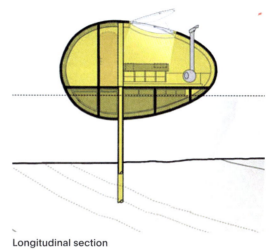

Longitudinal section

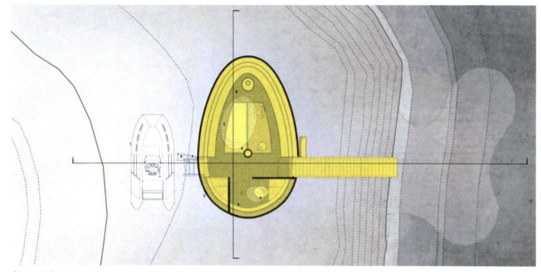

Ground floor plan

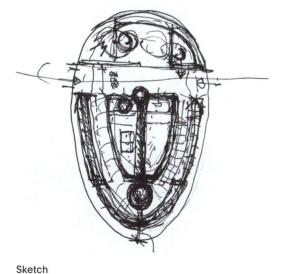

Sketch

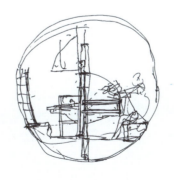

Sketch

Rooms: 1 room and 1 bathroom
Country of manufacture:
United Kingdom
Main materials: timber,
reclaimed cedar
Setting: registered as a boat

Index

2BY4-ARCHITECTS
Island House
www.2by4.nl
p. 182

AALTO UNIVERSITY WOOD PROGRAM
Kokoon Modular Living System
www.woodprogram.fi
p. 066

ÁBATON
ÁPH80
www.abaton.es
p. 032

ADD A ROOM
minihuset ONE+
www.addaroom.dk
p. 084

APPLETON & DOMINGOS ARQUITECTOS
Treehouse Riga
www.appletondomingos.pt
p. 116

ATELIER OSLO
Cabin Norderhov
www.atelieroslo.no
p. 108

ECOSPACE STUDIOS
The Spinney House
www.ecospacestudios.de
p. 228

ROBIN FALCK
Nido
www.robinfalck.com
p. 146

FAM ARCHITEKTI
Lake Cabin
www.famarchitekti.cz
p. 014

IPT ARCHITECTS WITH ECOSPACE STUDIOS
Aggie House
www.iptarch.co.uk
www.ecospacestudios.de
p. 158

JAMES & MAU
Tarifa House
www.jamesandmau.com
p. 072

JARMUND/VIGSNÆS AS ARKITEKTER MNAL
Writers' Cottage 2
www.jva.no
p. 122

MIMA ARCHITECTS
MIMA House
www.mimahousing.com
p. 248

MIMA ARCHITECTS
MIMA Light
www.mimahousing.com
p. 026

MOODBUILDERS
Heijmans ONE
www.moodbuilders.nl
p. 198

MORK ULNES ARCHITECTS
Moose Road
www.morkulnes.com
p. 234

MYCC ARCHITECTURE OFFICE
JP House
www.mycc.es
p. 242

OFIS ARCHITECTS
Winter Cabin on Mount Kanin
www.ofis-a.si
p. 008

OFIS ARCHITECTS AND AKT II
Alpine Shelter Skuta
www.ofis-a.si
p. 252

JAANUS ORGUSAAR/BOREALIS
NOA Cabin
www.jaanusorgusaar.com
p. 102

IVAN OVCHINNIKOV, DUBLDOM
DD 16
www.dubldom.com
p. 058

PAD STUDIO
Exbury Egg
www.padstudio.co.uk
p. 258

REIULF RAMSTAD ARKITEKTER
Micro Cluster Cabins
www.reiulframstadarchitects.com
p. 052

REIULF RAMSTAD ARKITEKTER
Mono-View Cottage
www.reiulframstadarchitects.com
p. 188

Index

RAUMHOCHROSEN – HEIKE SCHLAUCH AND ROBERT FABACH
Tom's Hütte
www.raumhochrosen.com
p. 210

SUMMARY – SAMUEL GONÇALVES
GOMOS #1
www.summary.pt
p. 134

THAM & VIDEGÅRD ARKITEKTER
House Husarö
www.tvark.se
p. 140

UNIVERSITY OF COLORADO DENVER, COLORADOBUILDINGWORKSHOP
Colorado Micro-Cabins
www.coloradobuildingworkshop.com
p. 096

GEOFFREY C. WARNER, AIA, ALCHEMY
Sonoma weeHouse®
www.weehouse.com
p. 090

WHITE ARKITEKTER
Chameleon Cabin
www.white.se
p. 128

The Deutsche Nationalbibliothek lists this publication
in the Deutsche Nationalbibliografie; detailed
bibliographic data are available on the Internet at
http://dnb.dnb.de

ISBN 978-3-03768-227-2
© 2018 by Braun Publishing AG
www.braun-publishing.ch

1st edition 2018

Editor: Sibylle Kramer
Editorial staff and layout:
María Barrera del Amo, Alessia Calabrò
Translation: Cosima Talhouni
Graphic concept: Edwin van Gelder, Mainstudio
Reproduction: Bild1Druck GmbH, Berlin

All of the information in this volume has been com-
piled to the best of the editor's knowledge. It is based
on the information provided to the publisher by the
architects' and designers' offices and excludes any
liability. The publisher assumes no responsibility for
its accuracy or completeness as well as copyright
discrepancies and refers to the specified sources (architects' and designers' offices). All rights to
the photographs are property of the photographer
(please refer to the picture credits).

Cover front (from left to right, from above to below):
Frederik Vercrysse; Juan Baraja; Olivier Blouin;
Bruce Darmonte; Janez Martincic; Add a Room, Johan
Robach and Matti Marttinen
Cover back: Juan Baraja